Strategic Internal Communication

Second edition

Strategic Internal Communication

How to build employee engagement and performance

David Cowan

KoganPage

Publisher's note

Every possible effort has been made to ensure that the information contained in this book is accurate at the time of going to press, and the publishers and authors cannot accept responsibility for any errors or omissions, however caused. No responsibility for loss or damage occasioned to any person acting, or refraining from action, as a result of the material in this publication can be accepted by the editor, the publisher or the author.

First published in Great Britain and the United States in 2014 by Kogan Page Limited
Second edition published 2017

2nd Floor, 45 Gee Street
London
EC1V 3RS
United Kingdom

c/o Martin P Hill Consulting
122 W 27th St, 10th Floor
New York, NY 10001
USA

4737/23 Ansari Road
Daryaganj
New Delhi 110002
India

www.koganpage.com

© David Cowan, 2017

The right of David Cowan to be identified as the author of this work has been asserted by him in accordance with the Copyright, Designs and Patents Act 1988.

ISBN   978 0 7494 7865 0
E-ISBN   978 0 7494 7866 7

British Library Cataloguing-in-Publication Data

A CIP record for this book is available from the British Library.

Library of Congress Cataloging-in-Publication Data

Names: Cowan, David, 1961- author.
Title: Strategic internal communication : how to build employee engagement
    and performance / David Cowan.
Description: Second Edition. | New York : Kogan Page Ltd, [2017] | Revised
    edition of the author's Strategic internal communication, 2014. | Includes
    index.
Identifiers: LCCN 2017004276 (print) | LCCN 2017008468 (ebook) | ISBN
    9780749478650 (pbk.) | ISBN 9780749478667 (ebook)
Subjects: LCSH: Communication in organizations. | Communication in
    management. | Communication in personnel management.
Classification: LCC HD30.3 .C69 2017 (print) | LCC HD30.3 (ebook) | DDC
    658.4/5–dc23
LC record available at https://lccn.loc.gov/2017004276

Typeset by Integra Software Services, Pondicherry
Print production managed by Jellyfish
Printed and bound by CPI Group (UK) Ltd, Croydon CR0 4YY

I dedicate this book to my daughter Yasmin – may this be the first of many great projects for her.

✦ CONTENTS ✦

PREFACE TO
THE SECOND EDITION

This book, and the concept of the Dialogue Box, is the culmination of some 25 years of working in the communications field. I have worked in a variety of communications roles in Europe, North America and the Middle East, with travel all over the world. I started in journalism, writing news, features and editing a magazine. I have worked with agencies and in-house, both sides of the desk as consultants would have it. I have worked in service and manufacturing companies. The one bridge I have not crossed is from business communications into consumer communications. I have headed up corporate communications generally and internal communications specifically, and the one thing I have learned above all is that there is a significant difference in style and approach.

I started in journalism, and this is significant. My first break into journalism occurred when I literally walked in off the street and asked the editor of the local newspaper if I could get a job on the paper, to which he promptly said no. However, he said if I went to study journalism then I could work on a freelance basis for the paper, which I did for a year. Different times then! Perhaps today such things happen more rarely. What I learned as a journalist was to be objective, and always to listen to a variety of opinions in order to find the narrative that emerges from these stories. What I learned when I entered corporate communications was that while this skill is invaluable it is not really wanted. Corporate bodies tend to want affirmation from their communicators, not the enquiring mind of a sceptic; in other words, they want what people call 'yes men'.

Today's world is a little different, and while 'yes men and women' are still in evidence, this approach has to be left behind. The evaporation of barriers between the internal and external world means communicators have to engage in a much more open and transparent world. They need to engage. This is a book about employees, not industries and categories, and means learning to approach employees as people, not as job titles or 'capital'. To do this means to walk in the shoes of the employee, and ask the question everyone is asking: what's in it for me? This is at the heart of this book and is fully explained, so I will not jump ahead of the narrative of the book.

My personal narrative has been one of a fascination with how people communicate, and I have been fortunate to experience this at the highest levels of organizations. What I have done in this book is to put all I have learned in one place, and in turn I hope I have provided a stimulating guide to help anyone who seeks to be a better communicator in their work, whatever the industry or organization, whatever the role and whatever the position. This is a book about how people communicate, not inanimate objects or contrived stations in life. Whether you are a CEO, head of a government unit or an academic project, or just simply starting out in your career, this book will help you.

As ever with a book, the author owes many people along the way. There are very many people I could thank over the course of some 25 years, so I will restrict myself to the most personal ones.

First, I want to thank Martina O'Sullivan, who took up this project at Kogan Page in the first place and saw the potential, but has since moved on. Thanks also go to Liz Gooster, for taking this on and keeping it going, and to the editorial staff at Kogan Page – Philippa Fiszzon and Sara Marchington, as well as marketing executive Andrew Thompson. I am grateful for the help and support of Lucy Carter and Sophia Levine in bringing the second edition to fruition; it has been a wonderful opportunity to expand some of the thinking of the first edition. I would also like to thank Hisham S Al-Joher, Global Head of Internal Communications at SABIC, who has been a wonderful dialogue partner on internal communication during the writing of this book and has become a cherished friend. The most practical part of this book, the workshop element, I was able to refine through workshops with SABIC managers, which was extremely helpful to me, and for this I am thankful to Hisham and to his extremely able managers Salman Al-Hathy and Benjamin Thomas, who have been hugely helpful in making all the workshops happen. Since the first edition was published I have conducted numerous workshops, done in small groups, in Saudi Arabia, China, Singapore, India, the Netherlands and the United States, involving some 600 participants, and the approval ratings have been around 96 per cent, which has personally astounded me. The reason is simple. The Dialogue Box is a highly participatory tool that focuses on the participants' own organization and helps them intuitively to arrive at an answer, the famous dialogue 'word'! It has been a privilege and a learning to undertake this work in such a sustained way in a dynamic global organization, and I realize now more than ever how robust and effective the Dialogue Box is in reality. I give my thanks to Boston College, chiefly Lisa Cuklanz, for providing me with an intellectual home and an opportunity to share my work with students.

Special thanks go to my wonderful research assistant, Yasmin, who also happens to be my daughter. This book is again dedicated to her as she completes her studies at the University of Durham and will herself enter professional communications as this book comes out. I also want to thank my wife, Hanny, my biggest critic and best friend in life, and my son, who is always an inspiration.

I have two hopes for this book. I have tailored the ideas to be used in a variety of organizations, as well as the classroom setting, to focus the dialogue we need to be having with employees at all levels. We live in a very noisy communications age where everyone is clamouring for attention, and where often public and private debates can be very ill tempered; so my first hope for this book is that it brings calm and focus to dialogue everywhere. My second hope comes from a few years ago, when I first presented my thinking at a conference on internal communications. One participant observed that my thinking was very democratic, and asked if this was not a problem for many organizations. It was an acute observation, and I think there is an openness in the approach developed here; I hope this book helps to forge greater democracy in the workplace.

❖ Introduction ❖
Internal communications, employee engagement and cultural integration

When 190 people were fired by the British entertainment retailer HMV at the end of January 2013, upset employees found a new way to vent their displeasure: social media. The 190 firings were subject to a fierce Twitter storm with tweets being followed by over 63,000 followers. No more the discreet escort out of the building or the cameras capturing images of dismissed employees carrying out boxes of personal effects – this is a new age of transparency.

The HMV Twitter feed was a blow-by-blow account of how major disruptions in the life of a company, troubled or not, erupt in our social media age (Figure 0.1). The notion that 'good PR' can control the communications space is gone forever. In today's organizational and business world employees are your communicators, and you cannot take for granted that they will toe the 'company line'. You need to engage your employees, and you need to find innovative ways to have dialogue within your organization to ensure you are not the subject of the next Twitter feed entertaining and amusing the outside world as your inside world is in turmoil.

FIGURE 0.1 No longer listening to his master's voice: HMV Twitter feed

The CEO of BP deals with disaster, or does he?

'I have said all along that we will be judged by how we respond, and that remains the case. The strength of the BP balance sheet allows us to take on this responsibility. I know that many of you have questions about how this incident will impact BP, your jobs, pensions, and our future plans. We have demonstrated robust cash flow generation over the past few quarters and at the end of 1Q our gearing ratio was below our 20 to 30 per cent target range, at 19 per cent or some $25 billion. We can therefore afford to do the right thing, and we will do just that – our financial strength will also allow us to come through the other side of this crisis, both financially secure and stronger as a result of what we have learned from this tragic incident and how we have responded... The financial scale of our response is just one illustration of the serious way in which we are stepping up to our responsibility to clean up the spill and mitigate its impacts.' (Tony Hayward, Chief Executive, BP, *Financial Times*, 19 May 2010)

As CEO, Mr Hayward focused on profits and pensions, but how much time was devoted to understanding the psychological impact on employees and any sense of shared culpability? The language is typical of a CEO letter to staff, though he did give more information and honesty than one tends to find in letters to employees. However, this was offset by his emphasis on BP as a safe environment at a time when employee perception of BP's record was at a low point, suggesting the need to encourage dialogue. It also pushed some agenda points, such as attacking the media, which also undermines the credibility of the letter.

This book, and specifically the approach it describes – the 'Dialogue Box' – will help you to move your organization into becoming a communicating community that shares open dialogue to move transparently forward and to address challenges internally and externally. The Dialogue Box can help any organization that has an internal audience to communicate to, whether it is public or private, and whether it is a business, voluntary, government or academic. This is not a book for the faint-hearted! It will raise many questions and highlight the need for many difficult conversations internally, which may be quite different from the internal conversations you have been used to or that your organization has been in the habit of accepting.

This is a brand new world and a new way of approaching internal communications is essential for survival. This is not simply a book that tells you how to do something about it; it also seeks to challenge you to question all the assumptions you make as you go about the task of internal communications. Even if you find yourself disagreeing along the way, I hope you will find the questioning strategy helps strengthen your approach to internal communications. That said, I hope you will embrace some new ways of thinking as well, and more importantly some new ways of approaching the dialogue your organization needs to engage in to become a better communicating organization. This is a book on strategic internal communications, bridging the critical functions of communications and human resources and linking to the three-way process of internal communications, employee engagement and cultural integration, which can refer to both geographic and organizational differences. This is also a book aimed at any organization seeking to communicate effectively with their internal audiences: business enterprises large and small, educational institutions, government and public services.

The approach I have created to help organizations to become better at communicating is called the 'Dialogue Box'. The Dialogue Box helps companies to explore what kind of dialogue they need to have with their employees to address internal and cultural challenges, by breaking dialogue down into zones: intelligence, emotion, interpretation, narrative and dialogue. The Dialogue Box allows managers and leaders to understand the intelligence and emotions of their company, and how these link to the ways employees interpret events and information and the narrative that emerges within the organization as a result. The result is the end zone of effective dialogue. Hopefully you will find much of what is discussed in this book to be intuitive – things you sort of know about already – because the aim here is to illumine so you can make connections you may not have drawn before.

To enter into a realistic dialogue and get internal communications right begs the question, what are the benefits? After all, leadership can exercise its right to lead, get rid of many of those who don't fit in and amply reward those who do fit in – to a fair extent this is precisely what happens in various ways in organizations everywhere. So the answer has to be, is there a choice? Communications as a cost centre and just 'PR' is an outmoded concept, and today, in our age of interconnectedness, there are considerable benefits and real financial rewards to doing communications well, and doing it in a more engaging way to make the most of the talent and efforts of all the people in the organization. This is what the book is aimed at helping you to achieve, and there are clear benefits in getting this right.

The structure of this book

The initial chapters of this book offer some insights into communication and dialogue, and also provide, I hope, some thought leadership. Business management is often very utilitarian in its practice and approach. The communicator should be the in-house conscience, the philosopher in the organization, who is able to offer an objective view of people and events. These opening chapters are for communicators and managers alike to consider the ideas and thinking behind modern communication. The latter chapters are the practical chapters that teach the Dialogue Box, founded on the approach taken in the earlier chapters. Together these chapters should help you to think more effectively as a communicator and give you tools to engage more effectively in dialogue with employees, and indeed with anyone in any situation. In Chapter 1, I set the scene, lay out some communications principles to guide you and address the corners of the triangle – internal communications, employee engagement and HR – before addressing cultural integration, which I then take up in Chapter 2. In Chapter 2, I examine the third corner of the triangle and tackle the question of organizational culture in a fresh and provocative way, and then introduce you to the Dialogue Box. In Chapter 3, I look at change management communications, and the Dialogue Box as an effective tool to address change in your organization. Chapter 4 looks at technology and how this is changing in the digital world that is revolutionizing our communication today. In the next four chapters, 5 through 8, I explain each zone of the Dialogue Box – intelligence, emotion, interpretation, narrative – with insights into these areas, all of which will intuitively appeal to you and should draw the reaction of thinking it seems obvious – it is obvious *because* of the intuitive appeal. I am seeking to draw out many of the things you already know, and thus help to deepen your appreciation of each element. Finally, I draw all these elements together to explain the end zone of dialogue, and how you can use dialogue to foster powerful internal communications and improved employee engagement.

Questions

1 Do you have examples of Twitter conversations from your employees?

2 Have you accessed comments by employees made online? How would you categorize them?

3 Assess recent letters by you, your CEO or other leaders. How engaging are they? Have you experienced a difficult situation? If so, what was said and how realistic was the message and direction?

4 Before you set out on a new journey with this book, write down what you consider to be your view of internal communications. Note what it does, how it does it and what the priorities are. Also, consider how internal communications fits within your corporate communications function, and what the relative priorities, people and budgets are. You will compare this with how you answer this when you have completed the book, so be as honest and forthright as possible.

5 Finally, write a brief assessment of how internal communications is handled in your organization, and give it a rating out of 10, based on the answer to the previous questions.

01

The new organizational triangle: Internal communications, employee engagement and HR

To use the Dialogue Box, there are two very specific principles we need to grasp about communications in the 21st century. While this is a book about internal communications, it is essential that we do not silo internal communications into being about informing employees, or simply 'cascading' information. In fact, I contend that the word 'cascading' should be banned from our internal communications discourse, despite its fashionable appeal in the past few years. This is because it implies hierarchical communications, and also suggests a passive fall of information. I am looking for a more dynamic way of communicating, which recognizes how successful communication within an organization is 'up, down and across' and requires active engagement at all levels and in all directions. I will call this process 'infusion', so from here on, whenever you see or hear the word 'cascade' in internal communications, insist on replacing it with 'infusion'! This word demonstrates the need for flows of information, freely crossing professional boundaries within the organization, with engagement up, down and across the organizational structure. The triangle of internal communications, employee engagement and HR needs to be effective across the organization, appealing to both the professional and personal aspects of individual employees. This triangular relationship will help to change the organization from being a place of people at work to a community of people working. This chapter will explain some of the principles and trends that are driving the changing dynamics of communicating and engaging with employees.

The first principle to grasp is that all external communication is internal communication, and all internal communication is

Why not cascade?

Cascading has become popular parlance in internal communications, referring to the downward flow of information from the leadership. Yet, in fact, the term refers to the cascading effect of when individuals in a population make their decisions based on actions and information almost passively provided by others, instead of relying on their own information, resulting in herd-like behaviour among the individuals. It usually occurs when the individuals do not have sufficient information on a particular problem or are unable to properly process the information they have access to.

Take, for instance, somebody trying to decide on what mp3 player they should purchase. Often people will go for the same mp3 player that everybody else has, because they have little knowledge of what is actually the best one. They rely on information from friends and observing what is most popular with others. The buyer is led to believe that if everybody else owns a certain mp3 player and they say it is the best, then it must be the best. However, this information is not always necessarily correct and another, less popular, mp3 player could actually be the best.

Do you still want to cascade? Or do you want to engage, infuse and enthuse your internal audiences?

external communication. This is because each individual in your organization is a communicator, and they communicate with each other and to the outside world. This communication is both formal and informal. Thus any external reports or events impacting your image also impact your employees internally. Good news can be energizing, while bad news can be demoralizing. We live in a new era of transparency and it is increasingly difficult to hide things from employees. As the HMV leadership found out to their cost, social media is a new tool that makes individual communications more powerful, and we need to pay attention to it rather than simply fearing its impact on the organization or being suspicious of security breaches.

The second principle to grasp is that, essentially, all communications come down to a single equation: $C = IQ + EQ^{10+}$.

This is to say, communications (C) equals the Intelligence Quotient (IQ) plus Emotional Quotient (EQ) to the power of 10 and counting! This is not a scientific measurement, but gives a sense of the balance of intelligence and emotion. Let's briefly explore this a little further – intelligence and emotion are two of the zones of the Dialogue Box that we will discuss in detail later so I will just highlight them at this point. In communications we are primarily involved in emotional management. When the news is good, we want to raise the EQ to excite our employees. When the news is bad, we want to decrease the EQ and dampen any negative emotional response. However, it is more than this. The emotions are part of how we are engaged, and thus with all news or information we want to engage our employees emotionally, to get them involved and behind the mission of the organization. Simple intellectual assent does not mean an engaged employee. The flipside of the coin is that an emotional or happy employee is not necessarily an engaged employee – there is a difference.

Twenty-first-century communications: A changing paradigm

Having established these two principles, we can look at the change in communication paradigms that has taken place in our new century. It is important to understand the dramatic changes that have

IQ

IQ is a 'number expressing the ratio of somebody's intelligence as determined by a test to the average of his or her age'. The phrase 'Intelligence Quotient' was first coined by the psychologist William Stern in the early 20th century. Intelligence itself is 'the ability to learn, apply knowledge, or think abstractly' (*The New Penguin Concise English Dictionary*). The IQ is calculated as the ratio of mental age divided by chronological age, which is then multiplied by 100. IQ testing is done by means of assessing rational thinking and reasoning determined by a series of tests focused on problem-solving, memory and attention. IQ is often used by schools and employers to help show what capacity a person has to learn, adapt, think abstractly and apply knowledge. However, IQ is not the only measure of a person's overall intelligence.

EQ and Emotional Intelligence

The phrase 'Emotional Intelligence' was first fashioned by Peter Salovey and John D Mayer in 1990. They define Emotional Intelligence as 'a form of social intelligence that involves the ability to monitor one's own and others' feelings and emotions, to discriminate among them, and to use this information to guide one's thinking and action'.

To be emotionally intelligent is:

❖ to be aware of one's own emotions and the emotions of others;

❖ to be able to monitor these emotions as they happen;

❖ to understand and manage both our own emotions and the emotions of others (in a productive manner); and

❖ to use them to our advantage – an example of this would be self-motivation.

taken place and how these changes have affected communications, in part because many managers have not embraced the new paradigm and are working within an outmoded view of communications. So, let's look at where we have come from first: the 20th century. In the 20th century, the communications environment was typified by the following factors:

✤ **Hierarchy**: information was about power because it referenced the position you had in the hierarchy. To know something was a way to show you had power, and whom you shared it with demonstrated power relations. To let someone in on the secret was a way of showing you had greater power. This is all very much a top-down approach to communicating.

✤ **Information**: linked to hierarchy, the currency of communications is information, and this was traded on a need-to-know basis. The beloved maxim of the age was 'information is power', and so power was held rather than spread. The exercise of communication was akin to a command and control approach, as organizations sought to control the message and the spread of information to maintain command over events. Towards the end of the 20th century there was a shift as a focus was put on the notion that information cascades. This idea still persists today, but in truth it is still old-style communications thinking.

✤ **New technologies**: with rapid change in new technologies we saw how they were taken up in a craze of fashion, rather than thought through. There is an old proverb that when a wise person points their finger to the moon, the fool looks at the finger. Often, in implementing new technologies, there was a lot of foolishness.

✤ **Obsolescence**: the flipside of new technologies was the rapid obsolescence of these tools, as new tools came into being and themselves rapidly became obsolete. Words, phrases and information, all of these were made obsolete by new technology and changes in fashion.

✤ **Broadcast**: being hierarchical, communications was treated as a broadcast function. There was a notion of authority, a central truth. There was also the sense that communication came at the end of a process, announcing the completion of a project, the outcome of a series of hidden action; hence the broadcast/loudspeaker function. As a result, communications was process driven, part of an end-to-end process, whereby communication was an outcome of different elements of the process, always following in the wake of actions taken, rather than driving actions. In business, communication was product-based, describing a product and what it can do, rather than its part in a solution.

✤ **Corporate communications**: the function of corporate communications was broadly split between external and internal, with the former taking priority over the latter. As a function it tended to be servile rather than serving, with the head of communications doing as they were told rather than recommending or being a key strategic partner. In short, it was not taken seriously and the communications people were just the 'PR' people, eager to please and brought in at the end of the process. The communications agenda was dominated by the media and was about enhancing the image and fame of the CEO. The role of communications as functional was not considered part of the organizational DNA. Finally, it was a cost centre.

✤ **Audience**: the interest of audiences was the pebble in a pool effect, where the interest was greatest the closer it was to the geographical source. For instance, in the United Kingdom, if someone died in a car accident in Whitehall it was news on the BBC. It would need to be a carload in Scotland, a coach in France or a boatload in the Indian Ocean to have similar newsworthiness; I'm sure you can apply this measure to your own geographical context. Audiences were also passive, and needed editors and mediators to access and understand information and events.

Much of internal communications in the 20th century was really communicating about *what* we do. However, in the 21st century things have changed. The world has changed, so why hasn't the way we communicate? Many organizations are using 20th-century communications approaches to communicate internally to a 21st-century audience. In the 21st century we have to communicate to engage, explaining why we are doing what we are doing, and extending our reach to connect with each other to create positive participation and change.

However, the 21st century is also an extremely crowded communications space. We live in an era where we are transmitting information at 1/1000th of the cost in 1970, while the volume of digital information is increasing 10-fold per five-year period. The 21st century communications environment has changed greatly, and is more fluid and challenging. The outcome is that we will never be less transparent, have less information and be less connected than we are today. The hallmarks of today's communications are:

- **Interconnectedness**: we are all interconnected and interdependent, as nations, organizations and individuals.

- **Speed**: everything is considerably faster, and our deadlines, attention spans and the lifespan of information and products have become considerably shorter.

- **Transparency**: we have to communicate transparently, both in the legal sense and in the cultural sense. It is more difficult to hide information today.

- **Low entry cost**: to get into new business areas or public spaces has become a lot cheaper. In communications terms this means creating a new magazine, website or other media outlet and getting our ideas or messages out there is a lot cheaper as well.

- **Privacy**: there are increasing demands on privacy as a result, and a feeling of discomfort that transparency has become intrusion.

- **Surveillance**: there is a great deal of surveillance, with CCTV, online tools and various other technologies tracking our physical and electronic moves. This also has an emotional and psychological impact as people feel 'Big Brother' is watching them, and our every move is tracked.

- **Transience**: the rate of change and flexibility of attitudes and trends mean there is greater transience in our society, with people moving places and positions more frequently.

- **Diversity**: our society and workplaces are increasingly diverse, with intermarriage and other trends mixing up our cultural make-up.

- **Globalization**: diversity and interconnectedness are part of an increased awareness of the world, as we experience other cultures through travel, food, communications and various other means, learning and encountering things that happen or originate in other parts of the world.

❖ **Experience-based:** ways of interacting in society and communication have become much more related to our experience of each other. Our interest in a product or service thus becomes more based on how we experience it, and so we will pay more or less as a result. Look at all the coffee shops and baristas, for instance. Is it only a cup of coffee, or is it an experience?

The 7, 38, 55 rule

The 7, 38, 55 rule was developed by Albert Mehrabian in 1967. It relates to what percentages of our communication are verbal, vocal and non-verbal, and I describe this in more detail in Chapter 4. Mehrabian conducted two basic experiments:

Subjects listened to recorded words and were asked to guess what emotion was behind each of the words. They were given three positive words (honey, dear and thanks), three neutral words (maybe, really and oh) and three negative words (don't, brute and terrible). The words were all spoken in different tones of voice. They concluded that the subjects picked up more on the tone of voice than the actual word itself.

This experiment involved pictures of female faces expressing three different expressions (positivity, neutrality, negativity) and recordings of a female voice saying the word 'maybe' in the three tones of voice conveying the same emotions. First, the subjects were asked to listen to the recorded voices and guess the emotion, then to look at the pictures and guess and then they were given a combination of both the recorded voices and the pictures of the female faces. They found that the subjects gave more accurate answers when presented with the photo than with the voice. This was by the ratio 3:2.

There is much dispute around the validity of this study, and whether or not these numbers are correct. What makes the study useful for our purposes are the important points Mehrabian was trying to make. As he stated them:

❖ There is more to human communication than just words. A lot of what we try to communicate comes through non-verbal communication, ie when reading an e-mail or text one must rely solely on the written words since there is no tone of voice, gestures or expressions. If the sender does not choose their words carefully, the recipient could end up interpreting the e-mail/text in a very different way to what the sender intended, because of the lack of non-verbal communication.

❖ Without seeing and hearing non-verbal aspects, it is easier to misunderstand the words.

❖ When we are unsure about what the words mean, we pay more attention to the non-verbal aspects.

We also pay more attention to the non-verbal indicators when we trust the person less and suspect deception, as it is generally understood that voice tone and body language are harder to control than words. This also leads to more attention to non-verbal signals when determining whether the other person may be lying.

Body language or non-verbal communication

'The conscious and unconscious movements and postures by which attitudes and feelings are communicated.' (*Oxford Dictionary*)

Body language makes up most of how we communicate with others. Body language consists of conscious and unconscious:

❖ facial expressions;

❖ eye contact;

❖ gestures;

❖ posture;

❖ position of the body, ie where the person's body is facing; and

❖ tone of voice and speed of speech.

Often our actions can give away how we are truly feeling even when we are saying the complete opposite. We can also use body language to our advantage by mimicking actions of, say, a confident person to make it appear like we are confident when we are in fact not confident at all. It is important to note that just like some words can have various different meanings, so does our body language, so we have to pay attention to the context as well. Just because somebody has their arms crossed does not mean they are being defensive; it could just be because it is a comfortable position for their arms at the time or that they are cold!

What happens when the brain can't cope?

The way in which the brain reacts to different kinds of stressors affects us psychologically as well as physiologically. When we are faced with a stressor we feel we cannot deal with, the response to this is stress. Stressors can be anything from an argument at home or someone bumping into you in the street, through to impending exams or job interviews all the way to witnessing extreme violence and fighting in a war. The point is that a stressor can be something very small as well as something very big. Let's use encountering a mugger at night as an example of a stressor... One night you're walking down a dimly lit street and you see a person walking towards you. Your hippocampus (the part of your brain to do with memory and learning) starts to draw on memories (ie has this happened before and, if so, what happened?), the amygdala (the part of your brain that processes emotions) then uses this information along with other sensory input, like seeing the man pull out a weapon, and decides that this is a threat and yes you are in fact in a great deal of danger. This then activates the hypothalamus, which sends a message to the pituitary gland. The pituitary gland secretes adrenocorticotropic hormone (ACTH), which stimulates the adrenal glands to produce cortisol. Cortisol suppresses the immune system and increases blood pressure. It also releases stored glucose (sugar) in the liver, which in turn raises your blood sugar. While all of that is going on, the hypothalamus also stimulates the adrenal medulla, which releases adrenaline; this prepares the body for the fight or flight response. Adrenaline causes the pupils to dilate, produces more sweat to cope with heat from your muscles, and raises your heart rate and breathing rate (allowing for more oxygen to pump round the body and get to your muscles). Most of your bodily functions, like digestion and staying fertile, take a back seat during all this activity, because those things are not important at a time like this! You are now ready to fight the mugger or attempt to run away.

This response, also known as the acute stress response, has allowed us to survive. This fight or flight response dates back to prehistoric times, when we had to run away from hungry lions and various other wildlife we now see in the zoo. However, in modern times it is hardly likely we'll be running away from lions, so what happens if we don't need to fight a mugger or run away from giant cats? The process still goes on, even if the stress is a result of a difficult piece of work; the more stress we endure, the more harmful to our body it is since we aren't using this energy to fight or flee. Stress can seriously affect our immune system, fertility, memory and many other things in our body.

Internal communications is about communicating behaviour

A few years back there was an early internet sensation known as the 'Numa Numa Guy', who lip-synched from the basement of his home to an East European pop song. It was funny, and quite uplifting. In fact, the Numa Numa Guy was a great communicator because he behaved in an appealing way and reached out to millions, all from the basement of his home. This illustrates how powerful communications can be. On the other hand, his message was just noise, childish, which is why his fame was both instant and transient. Much of our communication is like this. Employees may have been entertained by an internal video or some story, but has it really made an impact? It may have made us feel good or happy but whether a corporate video or message has been taken in as part of how employees think is another matter.

I raised the issue earlier that an organization can communicate to make employees happy, but is this really the objective? We should not confuse employee 'happiness' with employee engagement. If this were the case, the easiest way to make many of them happy would be simple – pay them more to work less. After all, many employees don't see the organization as a place of advancement or even satisfaction; it is simply a place where they go to get paid to finance their home and the things that make them happy away from work.

This raises the question as to what employee engagement and communication is really about. It is about getting employees into a trade-off between their participation in the success of the organizational mission and what makes them content with their work/life balance. To understand how this works it is important to understand human behaviour as it relates to organizations, and understanding communications in the 21st century is not just about communications as traditionally understood; it is also about understanding behaviour.

How we behave is what we are communicating and, conversely, how we communicate reflects our behaviour. We need to understand that how we behave is itself a communication, and see that we are all communicators, constantly communicating through our behaviour towards others, our work and our surroundings. All our behaviours communicate something about us, and this behaviour can, for the most part, be read. In short, to understand internal communications and employee engagement we have to have a firm understanding of human behaviour and how it exhibits, imitates and impacts the behaviour of colleagues and employees.

The internal communications and employee engagement partnership

The Numa Numa Guy illustrates that a lot of communication is just noise or distraction, filling the air and media. A hubbub, in which we find we don't live in a communications age, but instead live in a noisy, childish age. Perhaps more accurately, in communications we are currently in an adolescent age, and we need to become adult now. The communication business itself needs to grow up. The history of corporate communications is that communications departments have paid relatively little attention to the role of internal communications, which has hitherto been largely overshadowed, even ignored, by external communication priorities. All too often what the internal communications function within an organization does is a process along the following lines:

- Internal communications manager gets told, 'We need a campaign' for employees.
- They figure out a campaign to show how 'we care'.
- They launch the campaign 'telling them we care'.
- The campaign 'cascades' down the organization.

And the result? It doesn't work; it breeds cynicism. Employees are flooded by initiatives, programmes, inspirational messages and the like, expertly generated by the communications function but somewhat lacking in merit. Internal communications requires better strategy, more experienced talent and greater resources dedicated to success. The communications talent in most major organizations loves the media work, the invites to parties thrown by media people wanting to get their hands on their budgets, and getting their CEOs on front pages and television/PC screens. This is all high-octane stuff, with deadlines to meet and external stakeholders to court. This is important work for the company, and is not to be underestimated. The external image of a company is important; the high-profile management figures need to have a voice in the media, and communications is, after all, based on relationships, and social events are part of forging relationships.

However, greater maturity is required. The communications industry needs to grow in its organizational role. Even in this media-savvy age, as noted earlier, often senior management regard the communications guy as the organization broadcaster, the last in line to be told something so they can shout out to the world what great things the organization is doing. If communications is sometimes regarded as the organization's Cinderella, then the internal communications unit is the departmental Cinderella, a very low place indeed. Hence, when it comes to employees, they are second-class citizens in the communications journey to the organization ball. Employees all too often hear what is happening to their company, even their department, from the outside world first. The missives fired from head office tend to be high-handed and corporate, treating the employee as an outsider or someone at the bottom of the food chain. Survey most organization employees and ask them their biggest communications complaint and it will either be the communications department itself or issues related to internal communications. This needs to change and communications professionals have to take a more professional view of internal communications and give it a considerably higher priority than they do currently, and also understand the partnering role it has with the growing discipline of employee engagement. The reasons for this are obvious, even if little noticed by the communications professionals.

First, there is the obvious need for employee engagement, since a well-informed workforce is a productive workforce. When employees feel part of the mission they work harder for it, and being treated as an important constituency goes a long way to achieving this result. This result is not achieved by continually selling the latest brand gimmick. Branding communications is frequently the corporate equivalent of repainting the toilets because the Queen is visiting. Employees don't want to be onlookers to C-Suite contrivance; they want to be respected as part of the company effort, playing their role in a strategy they are educated about. This means communications departments cannot operate on the 20th-century basis of command and control.

They cannot communicate internally in the wholly inadequate way most of them do. Today there are greater issues of transparency and interconnected behaviours that need to be understood as an integral part of the communications mix, and they need to be embraced and infused in the attitudes of all employees.

In short, it is time in the 21st century for the communications function to grow up and become a more integral part of the management team and decision-making, not just the broadcaster of the corporate message or the ones who try to paper over the cracks. When organizations have a legal issue they call the lawyers in right away and the same should apply to communications. CEOs and senior managers should be demanding more from their communications professionals, and at the same time treating them as full members at the Top Table. They are not the private fiefdom of the CEO, or broadcasters of sanitized messages. Effective communications today needs a more holistic approach. CEOs and the C-Suite should put internal communications as a topic for discussion on their next management committee agenda, and keep it there until they've fixed it. And who knows, the communications professionals might find they enjoy communicating well to their fellow employees.

With better resourcing, you can get it right and will achieve the following three objectives:

1 You will have caring communications.

2 Communications will be fully integrated into the organization.

3 Communications will have infusion – they will flow through (not up and down) the company.

If we are to take seriously employee engagement, human capital or a host of other terms, then we need to get serious about the picture we have of employees and how they are effectively drawn into the communications process. On one level, many employees do not share the same values as the leadership, or the well rewarded, of the organization. On another level, they do share human values with the leadership. Notions of integrity, honesty and satisfaction with a job well done can apply across the board. If people are being paid satisfactorily and feel their job is largely worthwhile then these other motivations will kick in, and they are part of what employees are looking for in their workplace. Values linked to the profitability of the company or the excellence of a product in which the employee only plays a small part, these are much less connecting. People running the company have a bigger stake in the success and have a more influential role to play in getting a successful product or service to market, so they connect more easily. Nothing like a bumper year of profits and holding stock options to keep a person motivated. However, even in these situations some people can lack the necessary motivation, and of course more is also expected of them because they have the position they have. Like wealth itself, these things are relative.

Partnering with HR: Communicating organizational values

One of the biggest challenges the internal communications function faces is communicating organizational values, which is driven by the HR function of an organization. Today all organizations have values, and these are codified largely along similar lines. Values are relatively easy to grasp. Both these points are evident when we consider some of the most commonly stated organizational values: excellence, innovation, performance, professionalism, results, quality, growth, teamwork, integration, passion, safety, protecting people and the environment, sustainability, accountability, courage, commitment, daring, drive, leadership, entrepreneurship, innovation, ingenuity, readiness for change, stakeholder focus integrity, honesty, respect, people, diversity, trust, human and cultural diversity, loyalty and transparency. And there are some missing!

Frankly, there is no great creativity in what these values are or how they are chosen. On one level, some of these are values we can readily identify with, such as commitment, respect, trust, loyalty and other human behaviours. Others are more specific to organizational goals, such as growth, environmental goals, stakeholder focus and the like. We need to see this distinction if we are to grasp the fundamental point that to be effective, these values need to be internalized, and this will depend on how close the value is to the heart of any individual.

Those that are more formal or organizational will depend on a different communications and engagement strategy than those that are more basic human qualities. Where the imagination comes in is in how these values are communicated and implemented. This raises the question of whether values are aspirational or representational, and whether they are reflected in the reality of the organization.

When it comes to taking a reality check, communicating values is hampered by two often overlooked barriers within the organization, chiefly silos within the organization and the behaviours of the leadership function. When I say overlooked I should add that many people deny their very existence, at least in their own organization. To address these two barriers requires taking a long hard look at the realities of the organization, and creating strategies, education and toolkits to help revolutionize the organization.

Taking silos first, despite all the talk about values, changes in communication and increased transparency, the dirty little secret of organizations is that they remain greatly siloed. The impact of technological and communication changes is perversely the creation of new barriers to integration and communication. Different organizations are structured differently, and functions can reside within different units and locations, yet they are often siloed as a reflection of the big problem all organizations face, whether they like to admit it or not, namely the siloed reality of their structure or business. The existence of silos represents inherent barriers and disconnects within the organization, which in turn create barriers to efficient and effective communication and engagement. As we explore dialogue we will see why communications is needed to break down these silos. These silos, the whole organization in fact, operate within a much larger context, which explains the need for a new approach to communications within your organization. As we have seen, these changes include increased transparency and the increasing impact of social media and other trends, all of which contribute to the challenging context within which organizations are seeking to engage their employees.

Internal communications, employee engagement and HR, as the three corners of the triangle, share a unique role within the life of the organization. They see employees in their job role and as individuals, and communicate on this basis. They also cut across the functional and professional boundaries within the company. They want to see more infusion in communications terms, and they want to see how they can cut across these boundaries, or silos, to be more effective. In short, they want to break down many of the barriers within the organization. To do this, they also need to address the other major challenge to open communication, and the most sensitive: leadership.

Leaders behaving badly

The other dirty little secret is that bad, and good, behaviours emanate from the leadership of the organization. If the president, CEO, head of department, or whoever is leading, is behaving in contradiction to organizational values, then their actions and words will reverberate throughout the organization, because their behaviours are viewed as successful or legitimate behaviours in the organization. This can range from an overarching approach to management down to simple mannerisms. If a leader has a divide and rule mentality then they will find much division further down the organization. Likewise, if the leader does not tolerate political games then there will be less politics in their organization. If the CEO smiles at some bad behaviour then that is taken as approval, while a public admonition of someone behaving badly will quickly stamp out a lot of similar behaviour. None of this is to make a value judgement; it is simply an observation of fact. Many leaders feel division and competition constitute effective management, while others may not realize the ramifications of their own behaviour, good or bad. It takes an exceptionally strong manager elsewhere in the organization to refuse to ape the behaviours of those considered as superiors by virtue of position. Communication can reveal bad behaviours, which in organizations means being obstructive, exploitative, manipulative and secretive. These are all behaviours that block communication flows, and thus block the transfer of knowledge and the creation of new insights and joint effort. Many people in an organization engage in these behaviours, which prompts the question 'why behave badly?'. The answer to this is clear, because in some organizations such behaviours are seen as a way to acquire power, get attention and gain position, or simply to play games.

These bad behaviours can be exhibited in many ways, big and small. They include actions such as keeping people waiting for a meeting to make a point, or power-play, using an iPhone in meetings to suggest you have other things to do, and interrupting people when they are speaking. These behaviours can be revealed through gestures and facial expressions, so can be clear if you pay attention to them, but often we are focused on other matters and don't necessarily see these gestures or expressions. These bad behaviours can also be part of a management style, such as a divide and conquer approach to managing teams or units. They can be seen in delaying meetings to deal with other matters, breaking a trust you have given in committing to the meeting in the first place. We have to be realistic though, since we are all good and bad and because we all have behaviours that can come to the surface under pressure, and under pressure we might have a short temper. Likewise, there are good behaviours that surface when we are greatly inspired, and so when we witness an inspiring event at work we can respond with a great idea of our own. If you indulge in bad behaviours, ask yourself if this is the way you expect or like to be treated. We can also cultivate good behaviours. These include being respectful, trusting and trustworthy, truthful, and showing commitment. We are behaving well when we are being supportive, helpful and engaging. It is also about being transparent and connected. Are there good reasons to behave well? Yes, because when we do we are reaching into our inner good and human spirit, but more than this we unleash the full power of our inner self and we can inspire others.

These three issues of values, silos and leadership are at the root of devising any successful strategy to improve internal communications, and require a lot of self-reflection by organizational leadership to understand their role and influence in these terms. Before entering into a sustained dialogue, it is essential that the leadership at all levels is able to reflect sincerely on these issues and approach the dialogue with a sense of realism and openness.

What are the benefits of effective internal communications?

As I stated in the introduction, there are clear benefits to getting internal communications right, so let's be clear on just what these benefits are. One key benefit is in forging the knowledge organization that many organizations strive to be. This is because communications is a cornerstone of knowledge management. To know is to be transparent, which means being open to others. Transparency also means openly sharing, not hoarding or selectively sharing. In this way, sharing creates new knowledge as we pool our knowledge, experience and intelligence, and unleashes the full potential of employees.

Another benefit is to stop wasting the money you spend on ineffective communications. When someone is communicating we can ask whether they are informing or influencing. Informing suggests a degree of fact and objectivity, while influencing suggests there is greater malleability of the data and perception. Either way we are connecting, and our task is to assess how we are being connected. This can mean we are being inspired or encouraged to do something, or alternatively manipulated to do another's bidding, and the task of a successful internal communications strategy is clearly to achieve the former. Our most effective form of communication is face to face, but of course this is not always practical. As a result, most of our communication is mediated by passing on data through others and the tools we use, but is the message fully engaging? Like the famous, no doubt apocryphal, wartime story of the transmuted message whereby 'Send reinforcements. We are going to advance' from the front line reached headquarters as 'Send three and fourpence. We are going to a dance'. Ask yourself, is your organization advancing or dancing?

Communications rooted in focused dialogue can improve the group dynamics that exist in varying ways across your organization, as people decide what to say about whom, and in front of whom. People talk behind each other's backs, or will not be critical of someone in public, or may praise someone publicly for a private agenda. All sorts of group dynamics are in play here. The outcome of these dynamics is that we are creating a communications space, where the dialogue can twist and turn according to a variety of factors and the attitude of the dialogue partners.

You can match your dialogue and communications to the needs and expectations of your employees, and this makes for more effective management. The big question all employees have is 'What's in it for me?' This is not intended as a value judgement; it is simply a matter of fact. Employees want to know what their role is in the organization, what expectations others have of them, and how they will be affected by decisions and changes within the organization. In the case of a merger or takeover you will invariably find that the internal audiences become considerably more settled when the new organizational chart is announced. In the life of an organization there are different expectations, depending upon one's role, commitment and reward as a participant in the organization. For instance, a senior manager with stock options will have different expectations placed upon them than a teacher following a vocation. They also have varying degrees of commitment to the organizational mission as a result. Financial reward and status within the organization are the two key drivers for employees to meet with the goals set by the leadership. The task of communications is thus one of managing these expectations. This is not a case of 'spinning' although there is often a perception of this confusion. I am a great believer that most people are rational and reasonable within an organization. They should be approached as such, and yet they are often communicated to as if they are stupid or easily led.

Focused dialogue is dynamic, and in the next chapter we will explore what the Dialogue Box is and how it works. As you will discover, the Dialogue Box is designed to be reiterative, making it easier to communicate change in a changing world. Employees can be wary of change, especially constant or radical change, and it tends to unearth the trust they may have in the organization and lead them to question the benefits of remaining.

Lastly, good internal communications makes strategic sense. The seeds of success and failure are always sown at the beginning of a strategy. This is because the assumptions we make as we model our data and messages will largely have a fixed trajectory. This is not to say they only stay fixed or on a straight line – they will be affected by changes as we go along. However, from any given assumption we can reasonably predict a trajectory. This is often overlooked. If we understand the assumptions we are making, and their trajectory, then we will be in a better position to see where the strategy is going, and how to change course if there are new circumstances impacting our strategic journey. Let me give an example. If we make an assumption our employees are supportive and engaged in the mission, then we can see a trajectory of how this support and engagement will travel during the lifetime of a decision. If this is a merger, we can use this trajectory to shape our messages that assume this support and engagement and how this supports the mission, thus continuing to justify their support and engagement. If this assumption is wrong, then the merger may be impacted by the lack of support, objections from employees and attempts at integrating the newly merged company will be sluggish.

Infusion

I have already mentioned the term 'infusion', and we return to it here. Stop cascading, now! It's passive, hierarchical and does not inspire managers to pass on the information. The intention of cascading is noble, it is supposed to cover direct interaction, but I suggest all too often this does not happen or is not adequately done. This is because the manager doesn't have the time, direction or even skills to 'cascade' well and so the information stops there. Hence my objection. A cascade may conjure up an image of water flowing with energy, but in reality, organizational cascading all too often stops at the manager level, and have you ever had a shower that only reaches your chest? This is not to suggest information and messages should not be passed down, it is to say 'cascading' names a process that does not work effectively in organizations. A manager can say 'yes, I cascaded that' when in reality they have simply passed it on without adding anything to it. Some information may belong in this category, but the vast amount of communication for 'cascading' needs managers to add value to it, not simply to be overpaid data processors. Thus, passing information on does not necessarily mean it is being done properly, and the hierarchy of cascade means it is difficult for those employees further down the line to know if they have received everything, or that they have received everything they need to know correctly. Infusion is a process aimed at creating greater vitality in the communication work of the organization.

The 20th-century idea was the beloved maxim that information is power, whereas today we are increasingly realizing that sharing is power! The old idea was linked to hierarchy and a world where the currency of communications was information, which was traded on a need-to-know basis. The holder of information could include or exclude people by keeping or releasing information, thus showing who was in favour and who was not. As a result, power was held rather than spread. The exercise of communication was akin to a command and control approach, as organizations sought to control the message and the spread of information to maintain command over events and people. Towards the end of the 20th century, there was a shift to information cascades and this idea still persists today, but while it displayed the ambition of sharing information, in truth it is still old-style communications thinking. And the result of cascading? Surprise! Surprise! It doesn't work, it breeds cynicism. Employees are flooded by initiatives, programmes, inspirational messages and the like, expertly generated by the communications function but somewhat lacking in merit.

So, do you still want to cascade? Or do you want to engage, infuse and enthuse your internal audiences? Think how tea infuses. Now close your eyes and think of communication working through infusion throughout your organization; get the image? Infusion offers a more dynamic way of thinking about your communications. Infusion recognizes how successful communication within an organization is 'up, down and across' and requires active engagement at all levels and in all directions. This is why I call this process 'infusion'. So from here on, whenever you see or hear the word 'cascade' in internal communications, insist on replacing it with 'infusion'! Infusion is both a process and a way of thinking about communication internally. The key ways to approach include: training managers because internal communication skills are a core competency; supporting supervisors to be better internal communicators; providing interactive toolkits to support specific initiatives; having effective social media; having speak-up programmes to get ideas and information flowing; having communications e-learning for ALL employees; and finding your natural communicators, many of whom may not be managers or have an 'important' function. The whole idea is to define the messages and make the passing of information and messaging easier, which means finding and supporting the people able to communicate up, down and across the organization. This all needs to be done holistically, with training of managers and supervisors the key to the process and changing of mindset, and understanding that your internal communications is both a function of the department and the total number of employees you have.

Five steps to infusion are:

1 Clear messaging from the top, so EVERYONE can be clear on the direction, values and objectives of the organization.

2 A sense of story, so people can see themselves in the narrative, and where they fit into the story, rather than feeling the company story is simply about profits or what the manager does, etc.

3 When delivering information throughout the company, ensure the sender has made clear to the receiver what the information is about, why it is being sent and what is expected from the receiver. The sender is the one who knows why the information is being sent, not the receiver, so don't make them work hard at trying to figure out what they're being sent. Help and direct your receiver, so they will then share and infuse the information and messages in turn. If everyone in your organization does this, you will quickly see infusion at work.

4 Tailor information and messages to the audience. What works for a senior manager does not necessarily work for a shop floor worker or a supervisor. Different channels and different content will reach various segments of your audience.

5 Have listening posts, ambassadors and feedback programmes, so you know messages are being received, understood and acted upon. If something isn't getting through or is not working, then these programmes should be telling you that.

Organizational practice is undergoing tremendous changes today because of digital technologies, and this creates both a threat and an opportunity. The threat is that people are overwhelmed by information and messages, but the opportunity is there to get better targeted information and messages to where they are needed. Infusion is a contribution to understanding this and working towards solutions, but there is still much to be done!

One last point...

The corporate culture spoken of in management books and classes, and in company strategy sessions, is really the culture of the management and its dreams rather than something all the employees share, or perhaps even want. There is something very self-affirming about 'corporate culture' and branding that doesn't always translate outside the selves that are doing the affirming. This is why we need the Dialogue Box, to test the assumptions we are making. We can use the Dialogue

Box to understand what the emotional impact of a merger will be, to continue our example, and decide on our strategic communications. We can use the Dialogue Box to infuse our organization, because we will understand what they know, what they feel and what they think. Oddly, communications has a tendency to focus on telling the good news and believes that if only their employee audience can be told this good news then they will be happy! This is not so, and I am asking you to think in a more balanced way about communications, seeing both sides of the communications coin. There are all sorts of individual and cultural biases against the organization and good news. The Dialogue Box will help you explore this reality for your organization, and help you to construct more realistic pictures of your organization through dialogue for more successful outcomes. It will also locate gaps in the culture you believe your organization has, which takes us to the next chapter and a startling claim about culture.

Questions

1 How would you describe the handling of HR and HR issues in your organization? How effective is the partnership between your communications and HR functions? Where and how does employee engagement sit within the functions and their strategies?

2 Look at the channels you use (e-mail, intranet, magazines, etc) and assess how effectively you think they are used in your organization. Are you using these channels in a 20th- or 21st-century way? What changes do you think need to be made?

3 Can you recall a situation of fear both in a social and a professional situation? How did you react? What physical changes do you recall? Can you recall your own body language, and that of those around you? Jot down your observations and reread the section of this chapter.

4 How would you define your attitude, and that of your leadership or C-Suite, towards employees? Can you locate good and bad behaviours that seem to have a knock-on effect? What are the behaviours and how are they exhibited by leadership and their direct reports? How far can you trace any particular behaviours through the organization?

5 Write down as many comments you can recall made by colleagues and employees about the company and leadership. These can be both minor

and major things. Now categorize them according to seriousness, and also how long these comments have been circulating. What is your reaction to these comments? How did you respond at the time of hearing them? Are they things that can change? Are they part of the furniture of the company, meaning they are points that often erupt when there are times of tension or crisis within the company? Your answers to this will give you a sense of your organization's neurosis.

6   Think about how often managers have talked about cascading; was it all talk or did it work? Trace your own 'cascades' and decide if they are working for you. I think you will find it is not as effective as you thought. Now you have a solution. Think of infusion. How will this work in your organization? What people are in place to infuse, and how can you improve on the speaking up and listening part of the process?

02

Culture shock: Corporate culture does not exist

L et's get one thing out of the way before we proceed: there is no such thing as a corporate culture. At the very least, the idea of 'corporate culture' is not as helpful as the plentiful supply of business books and courses suggests. On one level, as a term of jargon to describe a range of management concerns, perhaps it has served a purpose, but it does not get to the heart of the organizational life. It is important to make this point, because if we are talking about communicating to everyone in an organization then we need to understand to whom we are communicating. Making an assumption that there is such a thing as an organizational culture is a big assumption, and one I contest in this book, as it detracts from defining an internal communications and behavioural strategy that truly reaches deep inside the organization.

The origin of the term 'culture' lies rather mundanely in France and in husbandry, but entered our common language at a very specific time, in 1869, and in a very specific place, the ornate Wren-designed Sheldonian Theatre at Oxford University. This was the time and place when the poet and critic Matthew Arnold gave a hastily written lecture in which he argued passionately that culture is 'the best which has been thought and known everywhere' and is a powerful force for good. His lecture was called 'Culture and its enemies', in which he launched a criticism of received ideas of action and the notion that we are 'too practical', as well as raising concerns about the rise of the machine in 19th-century Britain. That was then, this is now, as the saying goes, and today culture is a very big word. The word culture is now used everywhere, from the idea of 'high culture' of the Arts through to how we understand the life of business organizations. Today there are some 160 definitions of the word 'culture', and corporate culture is just one of them.

The illusion of organizational culture

The monolithic idea of a corporate culture is undermined by the reality that there are a range of issues of personality, class, education, religion, other beliefs, interests and self-interests that are simply too large and impactful to delude us into thinking there is such a thing as corporate culture. Now that I've dismissed this assumption, though arguably many of you may still have your eyebrows raised, where does this leave us? It leaves us understanding that we need to be much more specific about organizational interrelationships, rather than assuming there is a monolithic company culture.

What is critical to understand is that we are always communicating in context. Each individual or group is working and living in their specific context, and what is meaningful to them at any given time is affected by several variables. The organization may have great news to tell, but this may have little effect if other variables combine to dampen the news. The major variables that exist are knowledge, beliefs, customs and laws, which are part of human society as a whole, and these are acquired by tradition and learning. Any organization and its participants are subject to these variables.

Interestingly, in recent decades, scores of business books have made us used to thinking of business as Darwinian – a survival of the fittest and success of the strongest.

In essence, the term 'culture' has its place, but in a much more limited sense, not as something monolithic. It refers to something much more difficult to grasp, which goes some way to explaining why communications seems so difficult a task. Why are employees not engaged or excited? Why don't they 'get it'? These and all the other frustrations. To make matters worse, employees are flooded with communications at work, home and in society, all vying for their attention, and all having something to say about the person's identity. However wonderful your organization is, it is only part, and a competing one at that, of the identity of your employees.

Employees are not an organizational or corporate culture but a collection of individuals engaged in a range of cultures and sub-cultures, hence my rebellion against the much-loved subject of 'corporate culture'. Discussion of culture does go some way towards explaining us, but we are not an integrated organic unit in business any more than we are in our nation or other society. Culture is something much more open-ended. It is more cobbled together and borrows things and draws on many inferences in order to survive – hardly Darwinian.

I finished Chapter 1 by suggesting that the seeds of success and failure are sown at the beginning of any project or venture, in part due to the assumptions we make. The assumption of a corporate culture thus presents us with a considerable problem.

Because there is no monolithic culture, cultural integration takes place when there is an encounter between different people in the organization coming from their own context and point of view. The space that needs negotiating, the place of dialogue, is where people with their differences can learn to agree to a decision that is different from what they were expecting, or even remains at odds with what they think is right or appropriate. To illustrate the point, let's take the case of Sunday shopping, which goes against the beliefs of some Christian people who think Sunday should be a day of rest for religious reasons; a view shared with others who are concerned with the commercialization of the week, and who contend we lose something in our society by losing a day that is different from others. However, many of those who raise these objections may well work or go shopping on Sunday, having accepted on one level the practice of Sunday shopping. This illustrates the background to cultural integration, because this little example demonstrates how different people may object for different reasons to the same thing but end up as part of the change themselves. The same happens within organizations, as people learn to adapt to change. Part of communicating change is the give and take of participants; it is not a dramatic event but an ongoing process of adaptation and embrace of change.

This can lead to both a positive and a negative experience, as we encounter things that are different and new. As humanity, we are curious beings, who like to test our boundaries. As individuals, we can sometimes be quite the opposite, preferring our comfort zone and daily habits. In reality, this means some people overcome their comfort zones to make things change through their natural curiosity, while others curtail their natural curiosity and stay within their comfort zone. At some points, this can change, as people occasionally break out of the zone while some adventurers suddenly become very cautious. Collectively, this creates a mix of stability and change. Thus, change at work can be met with resistance because it impinges on these comfort zones and changes the daily habit. A move of office is a classic example, where the individual has to get used to a new work space, and may need to change their travel habits to get to work, the time they drop kids off to school or the store they pop into on the way home to pick up a couple of things for dinner. The organization may have lovely new offices demonstrating current success, but for many individuals it has to be balanced against these other considerations.

These elements impact how we use words, actions and tone to communicate, which is often context or culture specific. It is on the basis of our assumptions and interpretations that we each engage in dialogue. The way someone of a particular gender, race and class may speak to someone the same may differ from how they might engage with someone who is different, but we cannot simply separate these off in splendid isolation. A woman speaking to a woman may be of a different race or class, and may differ in age, experience and so on. Communicating to them as a woman is somewhat simplistic, although it has animated many a communications strategy in the past. New trends, such as the 'pink pound', illustrate the point further. While there are many homosexuals whose spending habits may align with this approach, we cannot assume that all homosexuals fall in with this, for many reasons.

It is beyond the bounds of this book to say more about culture specifically, as fascinating a subject as it is; the point here is to raise the overarching point that culture is more complex than often stated, and to suggest that organizational or corporate culture itself is an illusion. We do, however, have to deal with the range of cultural issues that impact the organization. In exploring the Dialogue Box further during the remainder of this book we will tease out many of the complex cultural challenges that face your organization, but let's turn now to the task of integration.

Using dialogue to integrate the organization

I have challenged the assumptions we make about culture, and this extends to the notion of 'cultural integration'. This is also a fool's errand, because although a company has a variety of cultures it is not the cultures we need to integrate but the people themselves. So instead let us consider how an organization can be integrated by dialogue. I've already discussed silos, but there are other disconnects within an organizational structure, and they start at the heart of the organization, namely the headquarters, which is also one of the biggest barriers to integration. There is inevitably a different culture at work in headquarters than in a far-flung foreign office, and indeed there are also differences between headquarters and any other part of the organization. This is because HQ is the centre of the organization, and its power, so it is a place where people see themselves differently from those further from power or out 'in the sticks'. An HQ in London or New York will in turn be a little different from an HQ in Milton Keynes or Albany in upstate New York. People working in cities like London and New York see themselves as working at the centre of the universe, the place where it all happens.

To integrate through dialogue means to recognize a more dynamic flow between employees and the variety of cultures present in the company, rather than taking a hierarchical or structural approach. While many in organizations today will talk about teams and engagement, there is still the enduring presence of hierarchy and the boundaries created by structure. In hierarchical communications, the trend has been to think about 'cascading', but this is a process that floods the organization with information and loses the nuance of all the things we have just discussed. How often do we think about communications about people? For instance, do we recognize different ways people work or who they are outside of work? A working parent doesn't stop being a working parent because they walk through the office door or factory gate. Nor do they stop because they are a senior manager or work on the shop floor. Information and images relating to parenting will be meaningful to them regardless, while young single workers are less likely to relate to information and images related to having children. Dialogue is about understanding the people in the organization as people.

All working people strive for some notion of a work/life balance, and this raises obvious questions about the kind of dialogue we need to be having. Should we, as Matthew Arnold's lecture suggested, avoid trying to be so practical and seeing the value of everything in terms of action, efficiency and profit? Or, can we see the organization as broader than these values, embracing the whole person in the organization, each with different ideas of what part work should play in their life? These are two critical questions for us all if we are to understand dialogue. They are questions that affect every single working person, because we spend so much of our life at work.

However, in addressing integration I am not denying the presence of culture; rather I am looking for a better grasp of its complexity in the organizational make-up. Culture may include many aspects, not simply areas of business and habit but also broader social elements such as gender, race and class, along with specific individual elements such as age, experiences, psychological make-up and medical issues. These cultural aspects can either connect or disconnect people, because they are the same or different. However, people may have many cultural connections but have a specific difference that is more important and trumps the others. Hence, two people may share gender, race and an interest in football, which allows them to connect on one level, but they may be disconnected by class or status, and thus the connection is momentary or fragile. On the other hand, they may share all these aspects but be separated by ambition or their role in the organization, which trumps all these common factors. In dialogue, we can connect with other cultures, learn about others, and thus integrate

FIGURE 2.1   Conventional 'cascaded' internal communications (this is not effective!)

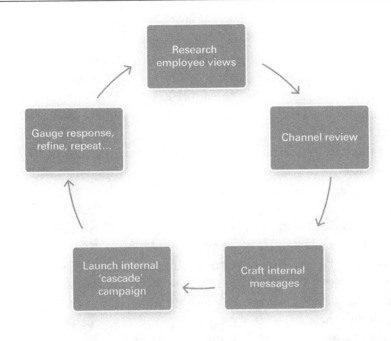

and interact in a meaningful and accepting way, since cultural conflict is often best addressed by understanding differences rather than attempting to create homogeneity, which is what corporate culture aspires, and fails, to do.

Using dialogue to connect

Part of communicating the organizational aspirations and change is how you use language. In past times, the language of business strategy was often dominated by aggressive and military language. The other dominant language is sporting, so we talk about the league we want to play in, getting to the end zone or hitting our targets. There are other types of strategic language, all aimed at giving life to the strategy, helping employees to visualize the direction and approach of the organization. The use of particular language is commonly aimed at 'controlling' the dialogue, rather than seeking a connection, and one area of major concern in communications is how we connect. This is also what we mean by integration, where the focus is on connecting to achieve a common purpose rather than for the sake of companionship or power. More than this it also means understanding how people disconnect from each other and within the organization.

To understand communications fully we need to learn what communications is all about, and this means understanding miscommunication, appreciating diversity in understanding, and realizing communications is not just about rational actions, words and decisions.

Miscommunication is perhaps the least recognized aspect of the communications process, because people are usually convinced that they are communicating perfectly clearly, and this leads to us overlooking when someone is disconnected, which may be our fault or the result of a deliberate action by them. We can all feel disconnected within ourselves from time to time, what is sometimes called colloquially 'feeling out of sorts'. When we have this sensation, we tend to exclude others or create distance from others or from our work, in order to protect ourselves. Conversely, when we connect to others, we seek to include others in what we are doing and also open ourselves to the approaches of others. If someone is or feels disconnected in our organization, it is the work of the communicator to understand how and to whom they need to foster a reconnection. We can best reconnect by being transparent to others. Others will feel they can connect to us if we seem open, trustworthy or reliable. If someone communicates in a hidden way then we suspect them of being political, or just lying, and so then we will avoid them or hide elements to protect ourselves. This is a drag on the relationship; it can never be as powerful because there are areas off limits or under-powered.

What we seek is communicative power, which is to say that it is about the words and actions of affirmation, recognition, respect and satisfaction. When we use affirmative words, pat someone on the back, offer them a cup of coffee or say they have done a good job, we are in various ways, big and small, communicating the things that we all seek. Yet in the words, actions and tone we use we can undermine this communication and also make power plays. The tone or actions we take can create distrust or fear, or be used to coerce someone into doing what they don't want to do or what they know is wrong. Words can be used positively or to abuse another, often in subtle word plays. The use of jargon or insider language can also be used to exclude others, because they either are not part of the profession that uses the jargon or they don't know the people or events that are being discussed, which makes it hard for them to connect. More than that, these word plays can be used to demonstrate they don't belong. Another all-too-common technique is mobbing, which often comes up in dismissal cases. This is where behaviour in a leadership group, unit or department can lead to an individual being pressurized and constantly criticized and attacked, hence the term mobbing. Under these circumstances, which are often moved by tone of voice or actions, an individual will make mistakes or just won't feel up to the job. They fail and are dismissed, ultimately because they do not fit in with the group dynamics, even though they might otherwise be exceptional at the job, perhaps even more exceptional than the people mobbing them.

All these examples are contrary to most of the values espoused by the leadership, creating a distance between the aspirational quality of values and the daily actions of people in the organization. Let's take a moment to explore values. Companies love to have their own set of values, and there is much to be said for them. However, how these values are communicated will determine how much they are able to connect to employees. Splendid rhetoric does not make values stick; it simply creates more communications noise. It could be said there is something insulting about how companies have traditionally gone about the business of values, as if their employees need to be told what their values are. The problem is often that the HR department went to page 69 of the 'How to do HR' manual and picked out a bunch of values that seemed about right. The point is, how are these values decided and how are they launched within the organization? The other point is that if you do a study of values across all businesses you will find there is great similarity, and if you do so within an industry peer group you will find they maybe have one value different from others but again are very much the same. The key then is not what values are chosen, but how they are chosen. The distinction is important, because we all have values and we can feel uncomfortable about being told what our values are or having them imposed on us, whereas in a process of consultation we will feel that values are being defined collaboratively in a more sensitive and meaningful way. Since the train has left this particular station in most companies, the main challenge remains how you communicate these values and engage your employees so that they embrace the company values chosen for them. It is worth considering going through a more inclusive values change if you feel the current ones have been decided too top-down. There may be an opportunity to revise your values in consultation with employees, perhaps reduce the number or change the wording.

Of course, organizations promote the heck out of their values, but as noted the problem often is not really having asked the employees in the first place. Again, the train has usually left the station in that you are asking employees how they feel about something they have not been asked to contribute to initially, but you can use employee surveys and polls to learn their perceptions of the values and how they translate them into their own work now that you do have them. If you have taken a more inclusive approach in choosing values, the next step is to ensure there is an emotional connection. We can all have an intellectual debate about the paragon human values, but learning to live them is much more difficult. How high-level values translate into the workplace is even more difficult. We know that broadcasting anything in internal communications doesn't work effectively, but this is especially true in values management. You're looking for a connection, a dialogue around the values, so that employees can participate in how these values are lived and continue to evolve in the company. This participation is not achieved by thinking that if managers shout loud enough the employees will live the values. Remember, values are usually chosen by senior management and reflect the leadership position and values, and what they think employees should value. As you reach through the organization you might just find this is quite a stretch. Managers need support to communicate values effectively and work with employees to find ways in which they may translate values into their work, with their specific context in mind. This means providing managers with adequate toolkits and training to live the values themselves and to become values managers who can encourage these values to be lived within the department, unit or team. It means finding regular opportunities to have dialogue on values, and to celebrate their presence in the workplace.

I'm sure most companies will say they have a good set of values and take them seriously, but I raise the question here of whether there is only a superficial use of values and suggest you test the depth of values management within your organization. This is no time for reheated rhetoric or pious proclamation; values are much more exciting for an organization than is traditionally understood. It's all about exploring the dialogue that will truly connect employees to the values, even if they have already been chosen for them.

The actions we take can communicate decisions more powerfully than the words in an announcement or the values espoused by the leadership. The actions we take need to be consistent. If we advocate a value such as safety but then put pressure on factory managers to take safety shortcuts to meet deadlines then we are acting inconsistently, so why should anybody listen to us? Certain cultural actions, or tone, can be important in this respect, as these elements connect us and make the words more powerful. This can give power to an individual 'lower' down the organization because they are closer in certain ways, and 'in their face' enough to become the most powerful communicator in certain circumstances. Let me use the safety example of an industrial company that has a major safety campaign at the heart of its values. The CEO visits the plants to preach the safety message, and the communications department promotes all the things that give safety visibility in the business. Now imagine it's almost the end of the shift and a valve needs to be fixed in a place up high, only accessible by a gantry. A supervisor calls over a young man and tells him to go up and fix the valve. The young man explains the safety mantra about wearing the right gear, including a safety harness, and to do that would take a while and he's about to go off shift. The supervisor tells him it's a five-minute job and the safety harness and other safety procedures are not necessary for so simple and quick a job, which could be done in the time the young man is arguing the point. In this moment, the supervisor is your most powerful safety communicator, who is in closer proximity than all the messages, imaginative campaign posters and CEO visits put together. This supervisor is close in role, status and cultural aspects, and most importantly has the full power of words, action and tone to make this young man put his life at risk. What would happen in your organization in an equivalent situation, and who can you trust?

To answer the example just given, and all the other points on organizational values, means having a communications approach with the heightened ability to connect people to others and to the organization, and by communication I mean we need to understand all the dimensions of communication: words, action and tone. As my example seeks to demonstrate dramatically, the most important and effective form of communication remains interpersonal relationships, communicating one on one where the full 100 per cent of our communication takes place through these dimensions. Actions are part of our body language. People physically see what we are doing. We can say we like someone, but our looks might well give us away. In addition, the tone of voice we use mediates our words. The use of emphasis, a sigh, monotone, all of these ways mediate the words we use. It is hard to connect someone emotionally with exciting words in a monotone voice, so what we look for is inspiring words stated with energy and enthusiasm in order to connect people. Or we use action words with a commanding tone of voice to get someone to do what we want them to do. It perhaps goes without saying that some people are better actors than others, so part of understanding this connection is that someone may be hiding their true motive, and using words, action and tone to manipulate someone.

Let's stay for a moment with the positive aspect of this point, which is that the way we connect can also mean showing respect. This creates a space for negotiating the first steps of connecting with strangers or new people. As we connect more closely we tend to drop some of the rituals of respect, or they morph into new forms of respect, so over time a handshake may change into a hug. We can show respect by speaking in a respectful tone of voice and controlling our actions. In certain places there are cultural distinctions of respect to consider, such as not putting your feet up and showing the soles of your feet. Shaking hands may be an acceptable greeting of respect. When visiting other cultures, we can show a lot of respect by showing we are aware of these differences and by behaving according to local cultural norms, rather than in our own ways. The respectful use of space is also communication. We all need our personal space, which is both mental and physical space. This varies according to cultural norms, where the distance we keep in a face-to-face encounter may depend on norms. There are many places in the world where people are quite blasé about personal space, while an Englishman dreams of an empty railway carriage. The most personal workplace space is the place where we work, which may be in an office, a classroom or on the shop floor. This means that arranging the office or factory space

Cultural differences

In China it is important for businesses to get to know each other before doing business; there will normally be several meetings where business is not discussed before they actually get down to business. This is because a lot of Chinese businesses are family run. In the West it is not so important to get to know each other that well; they get straight to discussing business.

In Japan and China it is considered rude to have prolonged eye contact. In the West this is a sign of confidence and integrity – not having prolonged eye contact is seen as being rude.

In Germany, Japan and China great importance is placed on punctuality. Appointments and meetings are normally arranged well in advance and turning up late could be seen as an insult. However, in Africa or South America it is more of a guideline for when one should show up to a meeting. In the West it is more acceptable to be late for something if there was something such as a family emergency that stopped you from arriving on time.

These are just small examples of some of the cultural differences, and they can be discussed at great length; indeed, there are whole books on these differences. What we have to be aware of is whether we are being culturally sensitive. Usually people in one culture will forgive, or find amusing, cultural faux pas. This is not the issue, though it is best to avoid basic errors. The real key is whether your point of view does not take into account the differences between your culture and that of another. This is where the problems truly start.

impacts employees, and communicates a great deal about organizational values. When there is a change of layout or a move to another building or site, this can be done in a very participative way, but it can also be done in the most damaging way. Keeping our distance can show respect, as well as look stand-offish. Likewise, moving people's workplace without proper consultation can seem like a terrible violation of respect.

Respect can also be established by ground rules or a charter set by the organization. Two examples will suffice. One useful charter to establish is for meeting etiquette. This can include opening with proper introductions where needed, a values moment to discuss how the subject of the meeting relates to organizational values, and articulating a clear set of actions to result from the meetings. We spend a lot of time in meetings, perhaps too much time in the wrong kind of meetings. Formal meetings for projects can often be wasteful because they are not considered important enough by some individuals who send along substitutes who perhaps cannot action anything or do not have the background to participate fully. Another useful charter is one for online communications. Among the trickiest forms of communication are online relationships, where you only have the words. There may be some context, and an existing relationship will inform your response, but there is always great scope for misunderstanding. When an international organization has English as a common language, misunderstanding can be common, because people are working from their own language as well. A quick example will suffice. A German writing English tends to be quite direct, which to English ears can sound brusque and even rude. It is useful when reading e-mails to be aware, and take a moment to think about who is writing the message. These concerns make the use of e-mail etiquette of paramount importance.

Dialogue as power

One reason why the pyramid operates in the way that it does is because organizations are social units of power, and are hierarchical. Moving from a culture of power to a culture of sharing is a key shift in our organizational behaviour, and dialogue can help expedite this change. There has been a discernible shift from hierarchy to teamwork that has taken place in recent years, and the attraction of this idea of sharing is that it values the contribution of the individual. There is still power, but it is changing, and it is important to understand the new power relationships, both formal and informal or personal. We have formal power relationships as boss or trainee, manager or teacher. This structures how we communicate by using formal means, rules and techniques. Some informal or personal ways of communicating personally may not be appropriate in these cases, such as a welcome hug or a slang word, which may be seen to violate the power relationship. Yet, these rules can be broken by those outside of the power relationship because of some other close bond, such as family, old school friendships, a common society or club membership.

Individuals are then related in group dynamics, which affect communications because they both reflect and impact power relations.

Traditionally, there has been a top-down flow in these power relationships, but this is changing and can be made more powerful by dialogue. We can explore power in dialogue, which can be revealed in how people decide what to say about whom, and in front of whom. People talk behind each other's backs, or will not be critical of someone in public, or may praise someone publicly for a private agenda. In analysing dialogue we can see all sorts of group dynamics and power plays in evidence, and find ways to create a dialogue that is powerful because it can connect us in the right way, or the way we want to connect. All too often what is understood as powerful is power itself, and so dialogue, rather than being structured to be powerful, is undertaken to acquire power over people or situations. In certain circumstances this is most appropriate, but what I want to look at here is how this causes problems within the organization and the multiple little power plays that occur every day. The use of e-mails and memos is the most common and numerous of power plays. There is a cynical view, not without some merit, that memos are sent to defend the sender rather than inform the receiver. There is more truth in this than the cynicism suggests. The issue is trust. We don't just share information; we are making sure that everyone knows what we are doing and when we are doing it, so that they can trust us. The memo can also ensure that blame falls in a particular place and someone takes responsibility, or perhaps ensure blame does not come our way and thus deflect from our responsibility.

In organizations, 'responsibility' and 'blame' are rarely far from each other. These words also reflect the idea of power within an organization, since all organizations have a power structure. How power is exercised varies depending on the type of organization and the people in charge, and how they deal with responsibility and blame. When something goes wrong the dialogue about who is responsible very quickly shifts to who should take the blame.

While the maxim 'information is power' no longer holds in the same way as traditionally understood, we still need to understand communications in terms of power. There is always a balance of power in relationships, with one person often in the leadership role. This is not to be understood simply as manipulative, though this can often be the case. People get different things out of a relationship that is based on mutual or shared interest but having a common interest is not the same as having a common purpose.

We now live in an era where power has changed. In the past we had old power, which is hard power. This is where A had power over B to make them do X. Today we can see that we have new power, which is soft power. This is where A inspires B to collaborate to generate X result. Certainly old power remains in places, and sometimes this is rightly so, but equally it also remains in places where it should not. There also remains functional power, which is defined by one's function or position within the organization. Old power is traditionally associated with this functional power. There is also personality power, which means charisma or charm that attracts people to want to associate with you or to do as you want them to do. Again, we can make the distinction whether this power is exercised to make someone do something or to inspire them to act. Another form is negotiating power, which is important because it moves people towards a goal. There are negotiations in terms of, say, a merger, but there are also negotiations in terms of ideas, relationships or goals. Negotiating the space is a key concept to the Dialogue Box, because dialogue opens up the space for negotiating differences of view, needs and wants. This form of power in terms of old power assumed a negotiation process whereby one negotiated either from a place of strength or weakness. In new power terms, there is a greater emphasis on win–win progress, inspiring the other party to do a deal, make an agreement or act based upon greater mutuality.

If our discussion of dialogue is generally focused on aspirational communication, then our conclusion on power should be focused on inspirational communication. We can see how power can be used for good, as well as bad, and what makes power effective in an organization is when it is networked for success, and dialogue plays a central role in making this happen. This is what I mean by powerful communication, because we are looking for group participation and the engagement of individuals. In communicating we are networking for many reasons; for position, information or achievement. Using a variety of tools, we network with friends, colleagues and customers. However, these networks are not technocratic; they are people-centric. To understand networked communication we need to take into account information flows, and see how and where information flows from us to other places and vice versa. How we receive information is as critical as what the information means, and will in fact impact the meaning. Receiving personal information from a stranger is a lot more problematic for us than receiving it from a friend or colleague. Likewise, receiving information from a connected leadership is a whole lot different from receiving an impersonal announcement memo.

In the networked organization, we need then to map behaviour, and an important study we can undertake is to map out how networks break down and create inefficiency. We assume networks are efficient; it is implicitly understood as such. However, there is always room for improvement and often networks can be inefficient. Like power relations, networks can be formal or informal, and often reflect power relations. Organizational structures and reporting lines are examples of formal networks, while friendships and neighbourliness are more informal, and very often can transcend the formal networks. As we saw with power, membership of a club or some other common interest can provide access that belies a person's organizational status, providing them with a line of communication and a place in the network not commonly open to their peers.

Communication space as a vacuum

We've thought a lot about dialogue, but dialogue is punctuated by silences, pregnant pauses and vacuums, and one of the trickiest areas for communicators to tackle in an organization is a vacuum. Often these are frequent at just the same moment as organizations need to be communicating most, such as during a takeover or merger, change of management or other event that has both uncertainty and dramatic change combined. These times of change are when there may be a high need for secrecy and confidentiality or where there are long periods where there is nothing for anyone to say, as decisions are being taken and positions negotiated. What is a vacuum? It is an absence of information, but it also suggests gaps or disconnects. Within organizations, especially in times of substantial change but also in many other ways, there is an existence of vacuums. Where there are such vacuums, we quickly find other communication rushing to fill the void, such as rumours, speculation and misinformation, all of which can be present in times of change, filling the vacuum caused by the lack of formal communication or a blockage of communication flows. In times of sensitive change, the leadership often tries to keep information secret or put up barriers to the outside world, especially external media, but this also creates barriers for employees. Telling employees usually means it is only a matter of time before the media gets the information, because the media will often get its information from an employee, or even from competitors who get the latest gossip from internal sources. Likewise information can be deliberately held on to until the last moment when there is a formal external announcement, though this may be done in conjunction with a 'leak' by internal sources. The outcome is that the majority of employees learn major decisions or information from the media before they hear it from their organization's leadership, and perhaps the sales force gets information from customers first or the shop floor gets information from union leaders.

In such vacuums, rumours and speculation emerge because it's just a part of our make-up. The challenge for leadership is that if vacuums are created or allowed they have to be tackled very quickly, otherwise they will be filled by other voices and messages, and then there is a struggle for control of the narrative. People are not happy with vacuums and silence, and the disconnect between events creates a demand for meaning. This is because we have a human tendency to seek to reconnect what has been disconnected. When we are communicating we are constantly seeking patterns, making up for blanks in our knowledge. We can see this in Figure 2.2. It is not just such images but information, events and other data that are pieced together as we try to make sense of our world. What we try to do is interpret the available information and create a coherent detail or narrative. In the absence of sense there are threats and opportunities. The threat is that there are interested parties who will try to exploit these gaps to foster a particular view of the situation to their own ends. Conversely there is an opportunity to build considerable trust when we take the steps that lead to reconnecting or fixing what is broken, and equally there is true leadership when we invite others to participate in this process. A focused dialogue will provide the space to address these problems and ensure that a vacuum does not create difficulties in the human network by creating dialogue to fill the vacuum. It is to the Dialogue Box that I now turn.

FIGURE 2.2   Perception: Making sense of what we see

Introducing the 'Dialogue Box'

Although we commonly think of how open and free the new world of communication is, with everything online and vast distances shrinking, we have also created significant new barriers with communication because we overwhelm people with information through a wide range of tools, channels and choices. It is increasingly difficult for people to see the wood for the trees. As a result, people erect barriers simply as a line of defence against the onslaught of communication both within the organization and externally. With the flood of e-mails and messages, new products and ways of doing things, many people are just getting overloaded and confused. In many organizations the number of new initiatives to communicate and constantly update, alongside the increasing volume of data, just grows helter-skelter. The loss of a top-down authority, as official communicator, means information faces the risk of being more chaotically released within the organization. This is a place where internal communications can play a major role, by helping to facilitate internal dialogue. Rather than being the broadcast function of leadership, the internal communications department should be a service to the organization. If the department knows who is communicating what and can orchestrate all the various communications about new launches and initiatives, then it can advise on timing and filtering of information. Internal communicators can also help by advising on effective communications so that various individuals, teams and units can do the job themselves, rather than handing it over to the internal communications department.

This process leaves the internal communications team to focus on dialogue, which then becomes the way to address this major problem. The challenge is to facilitate information and ideas exchange by putting the focus on dialogue, and creating a means of negotiating the space and conflicts between people and within networks. After all, everyone wants attention and thinks their project or launch is the most important in the organization. In times of change and conflict this is even more important, because people are trying to protect their territory. The important point to note about dialogue is that it allows participants in the dialogue to hold on to their own positions, or to suspend their position while dialogue is going on. It also means decisions can be made on a provisional basis, allowing participants to return to their own positions at a later point or move dialogue to a more neutral point. The advantage here is to allow people to arrive at a contingent solution, which is what I mean by negotiating the space. This understanding overturns the normal understanding that communications is about getting assent, which is simply attempting conversion, and as we know there remain many believers. I suggest we can use dialogue in a much more creative and consensual approach to your communications.

Chapters 5 to 8 of this book explore the zones that make up what I call the 'Dialogue Box', which is a simple but effective tool to help you address the challenges set out in these first two chapters. At this point, I want to make some introductory comments to introduce the Dialogue Box and its component parts or zones, and to explain how to use this simple process to break down any complex concerns your organization faces so you can better prepare your communication and engagement using dialogue by understanding its constituent parts. We have discussed so far the changing paradigm in communications; the Dialogue Box incorporates the ideas discussed so far and focuses them on five zones:

- ✤ intelligence;

- ✤ emotion;

✤ interpretation;

✤ narrative; and

✤ dialogue.

This is the new communication mix for the 21st century. Instead of focusing on tools, audiences and all those traditional elements in the mix, I want to focus on these five zones, which naturally incorporate these other important elements.

As discussed, much of our communications history is focused on intelligence, the crafting of the strategy and the message, and then broadcasting the result internally. We figured this was all we needed to do. However, whatever the deciders of strategy or information want to state as truth or the right direction is not necessarily what will be grasped by your internal audiences. The reality is that we all interpret objectively and subjectively, incorporating a whole host of assumptions, some shared and some not. This shapes the dialogues that emerge internally as a result of the decisions or actions taken by the leadership of the organization. It is a lot more fluid a situation than is assumed by those in the planning and deciding process or working in the intelligence zone.

When the leadership decides on a strategy it is also asserting a certain narrative. All the launches or initiatives that are decided and promoted internally are asserting a certain narrative. It is what we all do. We have in our mind's eye, or strategy, a certain trajectory that we expect the information and its embrace to go through. Just like the oft-used romantic image of two lovers running towards each other, we expect employees or listeners to run towards our message; the music swells, we embrace and kiss the truth. Unfortunately, real-life communications is more like a comedy version, as we and our listeners run towards each other, miss each other's embrace and then keep running off towards the horizon away from each other.

This is because communication is connected to something objective, which is a picture of all the interested parties and their own sub-narratives. An example scenario will suffice to illustrate what I mean.

It is one that I will use throughout the coming chapters, so at this point I leave you with just the basic elements of the scenario.

Imagine a company makes a restructuring announcement that they will close down one of their manufacturing plants, and will open up a new facility in China. A certain number of jobs will be lost and others relocated. This is an intelligent strategic decision taken by the leadership to ensure the company can compete and protect the majority of existing jobs. This, the leadership believes, is the best outcome, and they have considered other options in a host of meetings, a shower of PowerPoint slides and a cast of a thousand consultants. They have left no stone unturned, and they believe this is the right decision. They may be right or they may be wrong, and at this point we are not concerned by this; that comes later. What I want to establish at this point is the validity of the decision-making process and the conviction of having made the right decision. What the leadership has in fact created is a particular narrative. Like a story, it has characters and a plot, with heroes (the leaders), villains (the competition, government), townsfolk (employees) and a love interest (customers). We'll come back to this in the chapter on narrative; again I just want to establish that there is an inherent narrative, which is articulated in all decisions communicated and in official presentations and media releases. The leadership wants external stakeholders and employees to embrace this narrative, and this is where the problem starts. The media, customers and other external stakeholders for the most part will look at the narrative dispassionately and decide if there is a good story to sell (media) and if it supports the business relationship (customer), and this is done by argument and rationalization for the most part. For the employees, the concerns are much more emotional, as they are personally affected and may be unsettled by the change, fearful for their jobs, and so on. They will interpret events through the fog of this emotion, and different narratives will emerge that contest what the leadership has presented as the official interpretation and narrative. Rumour, speculation and changing events will all promote counter-narratives, suggesting other plants will close, the business is in trouble, or other stories told throughout the company. The question is whether the leadership's official narrative survives or is overturned by a counter-narrative, again irrespective of whether the management is right in their analysis or not. This is what makes the situation so difficult to manage and communicate through, which is where dialogue comes in.

Using the Dialogue Box you will analyse these zones of intelligence (eg decisions, leadership strategy), emotion (eg employee response, unsettledness), interpretation (the fog of events, different points of view) and narrative (eg counter-narratives, the dominant story) to focus your dialogue to address power, opportunities, tensions and conflicts present in your organization in a constructive and effective manner to deliver a strategic internal communications approach. The Dialogue Box is flexible enough to be used in multiple ways: to deal with positive and negative situations, for individual and group use, to address specific situations or create an overall strategy.

A foundational assumption of this dialogue work is that rationality falls short of wisdom. In other words, making the right decision and researching it well does not make the leadership wise in itself. How we engage with other stakeholders, present the event, time our moves, all of these can impact a decision and lead to even irrational outcomes becoming the winning move. The rationale, the planning, can easily go out the window when emotions take over, and this can happen at all levels of the organization. When we get angry with someone, suddenly our priority is having a go at the other person. When we feel wronged by someone, our priority becomes revenge or trying to deal with the wrong by involving others. Such things may only happen in a flash or they may be prolonged – it all depends on your anger management skills! The point is that sometimes the best decision or plan gets to employees by such an emotionally charged route that employees react angrily to it, regardless of how right the decision is, and the leadership is on the back foot from the start. The Dialogue Box will help you start on the right foot.

Questions

1   Does your organization talk about having a culture? How is this defined? Do you see cultures within your organization, and can you define them? Note down how many cultures you can locate and how they compare with each other, and with the culture your organization says it has.

2   Does your organization have silos? How many can you define, and how would you explain the relationships between them? Who are the individuals running the silos, and can you locate some opportunities to bring them into dialogue?

3   What major communication challenges has your organization faced in recent times, and how were they handled? To what extent was the challenge due to external and internal factors, and could the internal factors have been handled better?

4   What power structures exist in your organization, and how are they managed? Look at the individuals in positions to do something; how do they act? Those close to the decision-makers, how do they use the power of those they report to? How political is your organization really?

5   Vacuums exist when leadership is struggling or communication internally is poor, so what vacuums exist within your organization? What recent events have exposed vacuums and what sort of rumours circulated? How does the leadership respond?

03

Communicating through change, changing through communication

C ommunication can and does mean many things. It is also an every-day matter of how we relate to each other as persons. It is a basic means by which we cooperate and express ourselves, and also how we persuade, cajole or reject to get our own way or find agreement with others. It is an individual activity and also a function in groups, a business, government or academic environment. At root, it is what we all do, and it is fundamentally about behaviour. Communication is based on our behaviour and it is equally an influence on our behaviour. We can manipulate other people and events through communication, and we can ourselves be manipulated by other people and events. In terms of the organization, the important thing to recognize is that communication is not simply a function of 'corporate communication'; it is the activity of every individual in the organization, influencing and responding to events in the life of the organization. This means an organization with 300,000 employees has 300,000 communicators, and a small business of five employees has five communicators. They are influencing each other to shape events and understanding, and the bigger the organization, the more complex the interrelationship of communication between the organization and the employee. Things happen in an organization not simply in a formal process of communication, but also through informal networks among employees and in connections to outside of the organization. As we will see in the next chapter, all this communication has been digitized and has made our power to communicate so much stronger, but also so much harder to control.

For this reason, today, communications cannot be run by command and control, nor can it simply be done by the implementation of strategies and processes. As an aside, 'strategy' is one of the most overused words in an organization anyway, since much of what is explained as strategy is in reality short-term action plans or wishful thinking. This brief assessment of communication presents the dynamics that need to be grasped if we are to recognize truly what is involved in communication in organizations in our digital age. They are also the dynamics of change, which has become more difficult to manage because of the technology available to everyone. As a result, change occurs through communication at the same time as the change itself is being communicated. Our modern business environment is changing at a tremendous pace, indeed at a pace that at times appears to be almost impossible to keep up with and communicate. This makes change management a constant in modern business, and so change communication is a day-to-day necessity.

The people dimension of change

In change communications there are many major operational risks involved, and we also need to be able to look beyond the communications and available channels and see the human issues at stake. The employees may not understand the change that is happening or see the need for it. Some may feel uncertain or distressed by the change, while others embrace the change and see an opportunity for themselves. The attitude of leaders and senior managers is usually that change is either about improvement or necessity. It is the way to take the business to the next level. To employees in various parts of the organization there are other considerations, and they may not feel connected to the change. They may not feel that improvement helps them, and instead feel it will be more pressure or demand on them in their work. They may not see why a change is necessary, and feel there is just one change after another, often lacking in logic or direction.

So, let's take a trip down to the shop floor or a wander round the office cubicles and examine the most fundamental level of change from the employee point of view. We are all creatures of habit, but if you want to unearth someone's insecurities, or ire, then just move their work station from one part of the assembly line to another, or their desk across the room and you'll soon see what happens! Physical changes to shop-floor or office space tend to be the number one change phobia in business in my experience, and it is because whatever the changes in the business, the employee can feel more secure when their personal space or ecosystem remains the same. When they are unearthed from their physical space and routine, it affects them very personally and they may become easily demoralized. Such changes have to be managed with the greatest of care because employees will object even when their new setting is an improvement over the old. The old was familiar, it had a pattern. When companies move buildings to another part of town it impacts the home life; the routine outside work, such as time leaving home, dropping off the kids at school and picking up some groceries on the way home. I have witnessed company morale problems that could be traced to a change in office location. Office changes can be handled with good communications and can relate to a specific change in the future based on a conscious design, but what of all the other changes a business and employees face?

Companies today cannot take the approach that change is something that will happen in the future, something to be planned and organized without consultation with employees. Change is a constant, and for companies to succeed they need to foster a transformational organization culture, one that fits with the other cultures in the company. It means having employees able to adapt and to be ready for changes as they come along. Easier said than done! If a company is to have any chance of achieving such a state of readiness there has to be constant dialogue with employees so they feel part of the change from the beginning, and also feel more able to contribute something to how the change will be managed. To do this, leaders need to gain a deeper understanding of communication as behaviour. This means leaders have to communicate the changes taking place and those foreseen, while at the same time changing through the way they communicate.

This is the dynamic that will infuse the organization with change, and needs to be managed in different ways with different cultures within the organization. Shop floor workers, supervisors, administrators, middle managers and senior management are different cultures, and the people involved have different appetites for change and respond differently to the demands placed upon them.

We can use communication to educate, encourage and inspire each other. There are many levels on which we interact with others during times of change, which have to be considered. We've looked at a change in the physical space as arguably the most challenging, but a close second is when there is a significant organizational change. A classic example is a merger or acquisition. Perhaps I shouldn't say merger, because there is no such thing, only friendly and hostile takeovers! One partner is always in the lead position. One of the curiosities of a merger or acquisition is the level of suspicion on both sides of the deal. Even if one side is the 'target' and the other the 'hunter', you will find people on the more powerful side still fearful of the other. Some of this is natural, as there will be overlap and many positions will be filled by people from both sides of the deal. Hence, there will only be one Chief Finance Officer, Head of HR or new Head of Communications. As an aside, these positions tend to be filled by the personnel from the 'winning' side, because the CEO tends to want control of the money, people and message. Many roles will, however, come from the 'losing' side. These changes, whatever they may be, ripple throughout the organization and the vast majority of employees will be asking where they fit in the new structure and will they still have a job further down the line.

This then creates the most challenging and dramatic situations in which communication plays a key role, making change communication an important area of focus when we look at internal communication. As we progress through the next chapters, change provides us with the best examples of how critical it is to use the Dialogue Box, and you can look at changes in your organization that will best make use of it for yourself. Change communications can have a number of other contextual drivers, including:

✤ restructuring;

✤ new CEO;

- ✤ new or changed brand;

- ✤ improving customer service;

- ✤ incentive programmes;

- ✤ new vision, mission and values;

- ✤ changing market conditions;

- ✤ changes in legislation or regulation;

- ✤ a crisis!

These are some of the major organizational challenges where effective internal communications and dialogue can help to drive successful change, as well as reflect it, but they also create major challenges. Perhaps the number one challenge is that organizations operate in silos, for a variety of reasons, such as fiefdom issues for managers who want to protect their role, geography, unit or budgets. A merger or acquisition can expose these silos, and create a golden opportunity to tackle the problem. Whatever the case, it is important that organizations shake their complaisance and break open these silos, for they create barriers and blockages to the realization of full potential. The internal communications function can play a key role in this, by integrating the communicators managing the communication needs of these silos. The internal communications function should have as a priority the opening up of lines of communication between units and geographies. To focus briefly on the last point of crisis, good internal communications is a form of preventative crisis communication, because a great number of crises are caused by non-communication, poor communication and miscommunication. While there are many effective methods of crisis communication, the situation can be avoided or minimized by effective internal communication and the use of the Dialogue Box.

Change and uncertainty

As in a crisis, for employees, times of change are times of uncertainty, and may cause a crisis in their own work or life. In such times, employees will have many questions, and they may not necessarily grasp the strategic gain or necessity of any given change. They may react in fear to change, which is not uncommon. Employees may be fearful for their jobs or changes to their working life, all of which will depend on how confident they are in themselves and in the organization. They will certainly be trying to understand the impact any change will have on them. If we look at the organization as a pyramid, we can see information in a similar way to Maslow's hierarchy of psychological needs. The leadership is at the tip, and they essentially have all the necessary information and knowledge to understand their role; after all, they are developing the strategy, responding to the changes and making the decisions. They are ostensibly in control. The next management level is less in control, but they may have sufficient information either to know their future or to second guess what will happen. They are also making decisions, though they may find decisions they make can be applied to them as well. A manager may be asked to dismiss people, only to find themselves dismissed after they have done their task. Even so, they will probably have an inkling this is going on. They may also feel they have enough information to keep ahead of the game, either to survive within the new organizational paradigm or to find a new position elsewhere. The blue-collar worker, administrative staff and others will be at the bottom of this hierarchy of information needs. They may not have sufficient information to know what is going on, how they are going to be affected or to decide whether they should be looking for a new position and stay ahead of the game. They are not making decisions or exercising control in the new paradigm. They are essentially passive spectators in the change game. If we turn the pyramid upside down we have a better picture of the information needs of the organization, yet we communicate as if the pyramid remains upright. One of the objectives of this book is to help you turn this pyramid upside down and shake it up to see information as something that is processed in all directions.

When we look at the organizational triangle of internal communication, human resources and employee engagement, it is important to note here the role of these disciplines in times of change specifically. Internal communication means creating dialogue with employees, and if done well leaders will find their company will get through the change more smoothly. The very first thing to do is get to the employees directly and quickly to open up dialogue about the changes and how they will be affected. This is something successful companies need to do on a daily basis anyway, because those companies that engage well with employees experience higher customer advocacy by employees, higher productivity as a company and greater profitability. Internal communication is not simply a cost centre, it is part of the bottom line and it supports employee engagement by opening up the channels of communication, from direct dialogue to creating awareness of brand, values and all the other initiatives the company undertakes. Failure to recognize this leaves a company susceptible to more employee turnover, loss of inventory and more accidents. These pluses and minuses are multiplied even more during times of change. In total, companies who do this well will achieve two or three times more growth in their earnings per share.

Turning to HR and employee engagement, in the process of change management the HR issues become critical during times of major reorganizations. A company can invest millions in deciding the change strategy or launching HR campaigns, but if the experience of dealing with the organizational change or the HR function does not match the promise, then you're toast. You can preach as much as you like about how great the change is for the business, or how great it is working for an innovative company, but if the benefits don't match the rhetoric then you're done. Change involves leadership, and in times of great change and uncertainty, leadership becomes an act of imagination, not simply the exercise of power. Everyone knows a boss or CEO can ultimately have them fired, but this is not how you create loyalty or heighten engagement. The employee can no longer be treated as business fodder or just a number. The notion of the 'worker' has changed greatly over the last quarter of a millennium since the advent of capitalism, and while management books talk about employees and human capital in a somewhat high-handed way, we should seek a more realistic view of who the worker or employee is in fact. To do this we have to do a little philosophical digging.

The alienated employee

An assumption in the discussion so far is that employees can be made to feel part of the process, but often they are not. One issue is that you can't suddenly start being engaging and pro-employee. The employees have a memory, they know how they have been treated in the past. When a major change is made or a crisis occurs and you need input from and connection with employees you will be spending the human capital you have built up in your historical handling of the employee base. This is a different way to think of human capital, and a challenging one. Now, not many communications and management books tackle Karl Marx (1818–1883), but his discussion of alienation in the workplace remains enduring, and it is an idea that underpins some of the attitudes of employees toward the function of work. It is the idea that also underpins the analysis of cultural and political criticism which academics teach to many of the young graduates entering the workplace. It is also a significant factor in protests against some of the perceived failures of capitalism in our society. Alienation describes the sense that workers are people who are alienated from their work, downtrodden by the big bosses, manipulated by greedy capitalists, ill-treated by companies, and so on. The problem with this notion is that it doesn't tally with modern reality, but it does resonate to a certain degree, so it is useful to explore the notion of alienation a little further.

Marx argued alienation is about the meaning of the human spirit in the capitalist world. In the Victorian world in which he was writing, he argued that the capitalist mode of production leads to the workers having no control over their lives because they have no control over their work. Workers become part of the system, part of the machine, for they are simply part of the production process and are dispensable, thereby losing their autonomy. The idea resonates with many religious and philosophical speculations that we are human creatures wandering this earth feeling we are not in harmony with the world. We feel a distance or a sense of alienation from the world around us, but at some point in the past this was not the case. There has been a golden age but it is not ours, and at some point in the future there will be a restoration. The first point to take away from this is that the employee is a person seeking fulfilment in their life, not an automaton. Nor are the life and objectives of the organization their number one interest or priority; indeed, for many it is simply a place where they work and no more. Things have come a long way since the Victorian era, and employee engagement is pushing the boundaries with regard to respecting the person in the workplace, but we can do more.

Marx took his argument further by stating that human labour creates culture and history, and as such our spirit or zeitgeist is a human product. The practice of our capitalist labour, however, objectivizes our individual human will and thus we do not see ourselves in our work, and we cannot express our very essence in work. As a result, we become alienated, rather than able to relate to our work and others truly as human beings. While the workplace has changed a great deal in the capitalist economy since Marx's day, such conditions do still happen in many countries and businesses. However, to a great extent in capitalist economies, alienation has been overcome and modern employee engagement and communication practice seeks to establish a truly human relationship between the individual and the business process. Leaders recognize that people want to express their human nature, and many people do not simply earn a living or work to live; they enjoy their work and take pride in where they work.

There still remain elements of the Marxist argument that have become detached from their origin in Marx, which is why they have become working motifs in campaigns from across the political spectrum by anti-capitalist groups and in the more general debate in politics about crony capitalism. These social movements complain about manipulation by the powerful, alienation of the people and failures in what the economy should be doing for us. This is not the place to debate these movements, but we should recognize they are part of the business environment, and they do influence employees and share the debate about modern labour in the economy. They tap into some of the concerns and insecurities employees have, especially in times of recession. The presence and power of such protests can be influential on the mindset and morale of employees across the company. For much of the 20th century, changes in the workplace came about through confrontation, and it was a confrontation between the workers and the bosses – 'us' and 'them'. This is still true in many places today, though it varies across geographies and business sectors. However, the way in which we are organized economically today is different from the Victorian era, and it is still undergoing change.

How we are economically organized

Let us turn to another economist, one more sympathetic to the capitalist enterprise: Frank H Knight (1885–1972), co-founder of the Chicago School of Economics and teacher to a generation of

American economists, including Milton Friedman. Knight was one of the pioneers of the orthodox view today that profits come from entrepreneurial activity where profit is earned by forgoing current consumption, by taking risks, and by organizing production. This organization of production is not the manipulative process of Marx discussed in the previous section. However, he did argue that economic organization has both advantages and disadvantages. He explained that organization is near synonymous with the division of labour, with the fundamental problems being the assignment of tasks and the apportionment of rewards, which the modern economy does through free and voluntary exchange by individuals. The biggest gain, Knight argued, comes from the specialization and utilization of natural aptitudes and leadership. He explained that the largest single source of the increased efficiency through organization comes from having work planned and directed by the exceptionally capable individuals, while the mass of the people follow instructions. This is how he explained leadership in a matter-of-fact manner.

Organization also develops the skill and knowledge base of individuals. However, Knight explained that specialization considered in isolation is wrong when measured by generally accepted human ideals. He explained that it narrows the personality, and the specialization of leadership means that the masses of the people work under conditions that tend to suppress initiative and independence, which gives way to servility as well as narrowness, thus in general dehumanizing the individual. This seems to be an echo of the view discussed in the previous section that workers are alienated, but it is more complex. It is intriguing that Knight argues this way, since it can be argued that it is consistent with his realism that the workplace is not the place where workers are humanized; it is the place where they earn the money that allows them to be humanized in their life outside of the workplace. It should be noted that human initiative can sometimes create problems, jeopardize consistency and disrupt the process. The workplace is where we organize, coordinate and where necessary subjugate self to produce efficiently the product we all need or desire.

The four main tasks of organized economic activity, Knight explains, are to set standards to determine what things get produced and their quantity, the allocation of resources to the branches of production and their coordination, the distribution of the product, and lastly the provision for maintenance and future progress, understood in terms of resources, technology and wants. This economic organization and production also brings another apparent disadvantage, that of interdependence of persons and groups. The production of a loaf of bread involves the production of the various ingredients, the 'assembling' and packaging of loaves, distribution to the market, the invention of individuals who find new flavours, shapes and sizes to offer the market, and the interests and needs of the consumer in buying the product. These are various kinds of specialization that bring technical advantages to assembly and distribution, as Adam Smith had argued, but also create interdependence.

This is seen most dramatically in times of strikes or accidental stoppages, but most critically, as Knight elaborated, it is seen in the ebb and flow of prosperity, and becomes most dramatic with the recurrence of business crises bringing widespread distress to individuals and their communities. Thus, in strikes and in times of depression these disadvantages come to the fore, showing our interdependence. If the van drivers go on strike then the product does not go out to market, and if the bread company goes out of business in recession then the farmer has no buyer and the van drivers have no product to deliver.

Employee cooperation

Thus, the production process is not simply the selling of labour as Marx argued; it is a process of cooperation upon which we are all interdependent. Some of us have a better place in the process, while others are not so content. Some managers are well paid but very unhappy, while some shop-floor workers are content to do a job and forget about it when they go home. There are many people who find fulfilment at work, often at the cost of enjoyment outside of the workplace, especially when they are 'on call' or have to travel away from their families. For others, the intrusion of work is not welcomed and the workplace is simply a means to an end, where they walk outside the factory gates or drive out of the car park and leave all work cares and worries behind them. The role of the individual in this process cannot be neatly compartmentalized in the way implied by Marx's description.

However, we are left with the very real question of whether we are alienated, as Marx argued, or dehumanized, as Knight said. In Knight's view, the human spirit is not tied to labour, nor are workers exploited. People are badly managed, managers are often short-sighted, and so on, but these are the foibles of human nature and cooperation. Knight brings into consideration what he sees as a law of conduct and it is worth quoting him directly. Knight wrote that:

> When we are confronted with alternatives, quantitatively variable lines of action or experience, we tend to combine them in such proportions that the physically correlated amounts or degrees of each are of equal utility to the person choosing.

He is clearly not taking a Marxian view, and argues that:

> In the popular mind, and of course especially in the Marxian and most other socialistic literature, it is viewed as an axiom that the owner of 'capital' or 'the means of labour' has the worker in his power. But the proposition is false or meaningless if employers are in competition with each other and act in accordance with economic motives. The distribution of economic power in a competitive society is simply the relative market values of the property or labour services offered to production by different individuals.

Thus, labour is really a sacrifice of some desirable alternative to the use of one's time and strength. If there is no alternative there is no sacrifice, and so Knight concluded there was no problem to resolve. The socialist argument, he stated, fails to understand the relationship of property and labour within the system. People are freed from servitude and can form contracts, which is a great liberation. The spirit of capitalism, Knight believed, is one of being part of a constructive system, which replaced the previous acquisitive forms of economic organization, and which thrives because modern business is productive. He also argued that capitalism is the triumph of human invention and conquest over nature. The historical uniqueness of capitalist Europe is that it took technical advances of other civilizations and used them to lift each nation's status from medieval to modern ways, and eliminated slavery and servitude in the process. For Knight, the only alternative to capitalism is some form of servitude.

Knight offers an interesting and nuanced view of capitalism, which he believed to be the best system we have, but that it is flawed because we as human beings are flawed, which is why social planning fails. It is also why corporate planning fails! He has both a positive and negative view of labour. In his negative view, he makes the point about work being dehumanizing, and it can be, but not in the way Marx argues, and extends it into a holistic concept. Knight's argument suggests that we can improve things. He argues that the economy and society generally can only be improved by dialogue, in order to address the problems created by our flawed nature.

I have taken what I suggest is a worthwhile short philosophical detour, because if we are to understand communication as behaviour and the challenges set by how we are economically organized then we should be coming to terms with the fundamentals of behaviour and organization. Of course, there are many other views to consider; I have simply provided two views to spark your interest, and hopefully to send you looking into these matters in more depth. With some of this ground cleared for you, we can now look more practically at communication and change.

Improving through dialogue, not confrontation

The reality is that the workplace is continually changing and improving, and it makes sense in terms of production and efficiency to engage employees through dialogue as persons, and to find new ways to humanize the productive process. Modern management science understands that organizations are more effective in the productive process if they engage all employees in it. This also means understanding the objectives of workers at work; what motivates and what demotivates them as individuals in a function within the economic organization and as individual persons. This is best done through dialogue rather than through confrontation.

The basic view of most employees is they hope the company will do well, that they keep their job and hopefully get regular pay rises. Different workers have different skills, capabilities and needs, and their role in the company generally fits them. An unskilled worker is at one end of the scale, the CEO at the other, with various wages and packages in between. The less skilled they are in a job, the less a worker has scope for imagination or creativity in their work, which means the less the input of their personality is involved. However, the work a worker does is not simply the task they undertake, for instance being a machine operator or managing accounts. They work with colleagues, have lunch breaks, work in a particular environment, have employee benefits, and so on. The objective of management and organization is to ensure they do their tasks well, and they will do so if they are sufficiently content in their place of work and home. The management can do much about the former, little about the latter. People bring their problems to work, as much as they may have problems at work.

The more troubled or alienated a worker feels, and the less engaged they are with their work, then the greater the likelihood of accidents, poor productivity and even theft or damage of company property. A good supervisor or manager can pick up on such problems and at least manage performance at work as a result. If the employee has pride in their work and organization then they will be at the very least more productive, and at best they can play a role in improving performance by thinking of new ways to do things, and of course getting promoted.

We know that a business has to be run, and the process of production must be set to meet a market demand. Ultimately, even the best organizations have to lay people off or fire workers for poor performance. The reality is that the workplace is not about being a 'nice' place. It is about being a well-organized, productive and successful place. A part of this is recognizing that the well-being of employees is part of the success and the productive process. This is easier in good times than in difficult times. Managing employees in the bad times, or when there is conflict, is more difficult. This is still to a large extent done badly in organizations, which creates tensions and can lead to confrontation rather than cooperation. The modern technique of managing these situations and the people has become the province of 'HR', the human resources department. The HR function is often criticized by employees for being poorly run, in part because some organizations often pay lip service to employee engagement, and in part because they do not have the backing of top management to match the HR promise with the reality of the organization. HR is a difficult task. The HR function has to look at the individual as a functionary and as a person. This means there is great scope for human error in dealing with individuals. It means managing the emotions of employees, and we live in a society where emotional management has become increasingly central.

Dialogue and emotion

Managing the emotions and conflicts between employees and the organizational objectives is best achieved by dialogue, as it is in society generally. Dialogue is a very human activity, but we do not conduct our dialogues in a wholly rational way; they are usually touched by emotion. In good times, we manage emotionally by trying to get people excited about what we are saying, while in difficult times we are trying to calm people down or deal with fear and anxiety. Because we are not purely rational beings, emotions often block progress or change our priorities. Think for instance about when we are working on something and someone does something that angers us, and suddenly our priority is telling the other person what they've done wrong rather than meeting our objective. Likewise, when we surprise people or ignore their emotional state, they will not listen to what we want to tell them or respond to our direction for them to do something.

While we know dialogue is essential in many situations, not just at work, we don't always know how to go about it. This becomes a communication problem, and miscommunication and non-communication as mentioned above are frequent causes of mistakes and crisis. Effective dialogue is best done by understanding both the rational and emotional dimensions of a situation, and by understanding that people interpret events differently. When we think this way, we can deal with the situation we face by realizing that it may not be what we think it is. This management of people and the need for dialogue are the elements of cooperation, and capitalism is a cooperative process that allows people with different experiences, views and beliefs to interact and work together toward common goals, and to deal with the foundational economic reality of scarcity. While important, corporate governance, increasing regulations and other similar approaches and tools used increasingly in markets and society today are based on forcing society forward using specific principles that are often negative as a form of managing our organizations and society. I suggest we should have a more positive view that we can achieve more in capitalism and democracy by dialogue with cooperation based on understanding we are persons in conflict pursuing scarcity, and we have to cooperate responsibly through greater dialogue to manage our organizations and thus create, rather than try to dictate, a better society.

Democracy in the workplace?

When I wrote in an article ('Maybe your workplace should be a democracy', 8 February 2016) for the premier Canadian newspaper *Globe and Mail* that maybe the workplace should be a democracy, it didn't take long for readers to comment this was a bad idea. I was told that bosses and leaders run companies, shareholders decide, and all the other arguments came to the fore. What I didn't mean was that employees should decide things; that is part of the job function of leaders. Nor did I mean that companies should introduce some kind of voting system! What I meant is that organizations should be more participative and have open dialogue, striving to get more meaningful input from employees. I also did not mean the usual company dialogue where employees hear the boss say, 'Our people are our number one priority', or, 'We can't be successful without our people', only to find such statements are the first and last mention of 'people' as the boss goes on to talk about financial goals, business targets and other priorities. The point is that business leaders talk past their employees on a regular basis, and fail to have open and honest dialogue with them. There are many reasons for this, but the primary ones include lack of trust or authentic respect, and suspicion. All too often, leaders regard their employees as people who need to be told things on a 'need-to-know basis' because they don't really understand the complex decisions leaders need to make.

Leaders should have more confidence that most of their employees do understand, and are more trusting and trustworthy than is generally recognized. The point of engaging employees is not to spin the news or keep them happy by hiding troubles from them. If you want to make employees happy, pay them a lot more to work a lot less and you may achieve that. A better approach is to have meaningful dialogue that shares the organization's burdens rather than objectifying staff as part of the problem. Employees know their companies have difficulties to face, and will often understand what's good for the company, even if it is bad news for them personally. But they'll only 'get it' if you explain it to them in a meaningful way. In the 21st century, organizational democracy can help make companies more successful, because it can make for a workplace in which employees are respected, included and consulted. One where their views are heard, responded to, and even form part of the solution. This is the true power of the modern organization, where there is greater openness. It is only through open dialogue, rather than hierarchical communication, that leaders can unleash the power within their organizations. Achieving this requires finding out what is meaningful to employees in different parts of the company. This can only be done by understanding the internal audience, and by leaders seeing things from other points of view, because people in the company do see things differently and have different needs. For example, positive financial figures are great, but how financial results are understood or made meaningful to a lathe worker versus a middle manager or chief executive officer can be radically different. Likewise, when the results are bad, everyone is affected differently. Such results need to be communicated to everyone, but in a very targeted way if they are to be embraced and understood by everyone.

Having effective dialogue requires leaders to show more respect for all employees, and it requires grasping and acknowledging the emotional impact any decision has on them. Engaging emotionally with employees is critical to successful dialogue within the organization. This may be a struggle for leaders used to communicating on the basis of their 'position', but leadership needs to be inspirational. To be inspirational demands being open and listening, and I mean real listening, not paying lip service to the idea in those 'Our people are our number one priority' speeches. This is what real democracy looks like: mutual respect, understanding and open dialogue. As in political democracy, business leaders need to win hearts and minds. Leaders need to cast off suspicions and doubts, and start having meaningful dialogue with their people in the most open and transparent way they can. The Dialogue Box can help you achieve this in what is a reiterative process, because as the information in the zones changes so too do the narrative and the dialogue needed to bring everyone together in a communicating community.

CASE STUDY

A dialogue at the opera

The opera is not your run-of-the-mill employee engagement case study, but changing events at the Metropolitan Opera in New York show there is a great need for dialogue in a place of musical dialogue where the management and staff are very much out of tune with each other. This was a situation when the opera staff, including singers, went on strike and at the time this threatened the opening of the new season. I am grateful to *The New York Times'* reporting on the dispute. This Dialogue Box was published online at the time and it was read by parties to the dispute, but I am unaware whether it helped them. It is offered here as a case study analysis of how the Dialogue Box can be used in a change dispute which involved a strike, the ultimate confrontation between management and employees. Either way, the problem was happily resolved.

How would the Dialogue Box approach the matter? There are five zones to the Dialogue Box: intelligence, emotion, interpretation, narrative and, finally, dialogue. We are studying how the Dialogue Box seeks to locate the heart of the challenge in each zone, and use this to define the dialogue word that could create effective dialogue to change the situation, in this case to bring parties in dispute from a broken relationship to a more engaging approach to solving the problem.

Intelligence: In the intelligence zone, the Dialogue Box simply sets out what the position is and what decision management is seeking to take to employees. There is no judgement involved as to whether this is the right or wrong way to start, it is simply assuming a starting place for analysing dialogue.

In the Met Opera Intelligence Zone: The Met Opera is facing severe financial difficulties and has decided it needs to reduce labour costs. A new contract deal is on the table, which involves a cut in pay and benefits. Peter Gelb, the general manager, has sent the company's orchestra, chorus, stagehands and other workers letters warning them to prepare for a lockout if no contract deal is reached by the following week. A deadline was set for 1 August, and Mr Gelb said, 'I sincerely hope to avoid such an unfortunate event.'

Emotion: The emotion zone defines the emotional state of employees in response to the intelligence they have received from management.

In the Met Opera Emotion Zone: The emotional response from employees is recorded as one of dismay and they are unsettled about the forthcoming season and their future.

Interpretation: The interpretation zone assesses what sort of interpretation employees will have of any actions, decisions or words offered by management following the release of the intelligence and after the emotional response.

In the Met Opera Interpretation Zone: The current way employees are interpreting any actions by Mr Gelb is that he is acting cynically and they feel alienated.

Narrative: The narrative zone defines the narrative, which is a counter-narrative to the management narrative that they were attempting to define the problem of cost cutting to save the Met Opera and secure its future.

In the Met Opera Narrative Zone: The Met Opera management has stated it needs to cut costs to secure its future. But, in the current state of negotiation there is no chance the employees and management can reach an agreement, because employees believe that management is intransigent. If there is no agreement, the new season will not open.

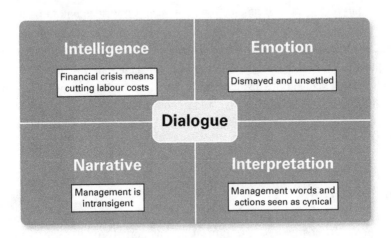

So, we have a clear counter-narrative. The management believes cost cuts are needed to secure the future, but employees dispute this and the deadline is looming in a state of deadlock. What dialogue word is needed to unblock this state of affairs and find a way out of the deadlock?

Back in 1980, there was an 11-week lockout that delayed the opening season until December, and apart from sales it had a knock-on effect on other forms of giving that the Met Opera relies on. This is a no-win situation. As *The New York Times* reported, 'A lockout would have perils for both sides.' So, how do we negotiate a win for both sides? The starting point is finding a dialogue word that both sides can relate to, one which can guide and benchmark the dialogue.

What dialogue word? Answers come out of dialogue workshops, and are not easily defined from a distance. In addition, the Dialogue Box is partly about the process of analysing the problem more fully; it is a creative process at work. This is one dialogue I would love to have been involved in, but I can offer a view on where I could see this dialogue going, and there are two routes to consider. First is a word that would be somewhere on the theme of cooperation. I would explore this, but given the acrimony surrounding this dispute, we may not have gone very far down this road.

This dialogue needed to be solved to allow opening night on 22 September, with a new production of Mozart's *Le nozze di Figaro* an opera buffa which recounts a single 'day of madness' (*la folle journée*). This may be pertinent, and offers a dialogue word I suggested the Met Opera explore: madness. The narrative the dispute was following at the time suggested madness, because the new season not opening would not secure its future, while employees believed the level of cost cutting was madness in their eyes. On this basis, we find a word that is meaningful to both sides, and they would be talking about the same thing, even if it has different impacts from each point of view. Both sides had to realize the madness of the situation to solve it together, and happily for opera goers it was solved and the season opened as planned. You can find a full report on the dispute by James B Stewart in 'A fight at the opera' published in *The New Yorker* (23 March 2015). I suggest the dispute would have been solved sooner if they had used the Dialogue Box in what was a very confrontational situation. As a case study, you could use this to discern what advice you might have given at the time.

Questions

1 Look at the changes your organization has gone through, or is going through now, and analyse how well you think change is communicated in your organization and by your leadership. Are changes explained well? Are employees clearly guided through the process and steps involved?

2 How would you describe the communication behaviours of your leaders?

3 If the hierarchy of communication concept was applied to your organization, what would it look like?

4 Do you agree workers are alienated, and if so does the discontent expressed by protest and other groups outside affect those inside your company?

5 What do you see as the motivation of people in your organization? How would you explain this at different levels of the organization, from the C-suite to the shop floor?

6 Are there high levels of cooperation in your organization? What means do people in your organization use that prevent or promote cooperation?

7 How would you describe the level and process of engagement with employees in your organization? What would an engagement map look like in your organization?

8 Think of crises or problems that have occurred in your organizations. Which ones and how many can you trace back to poor communication, miscommunication and non-communication? What can you learn from this?

9 Do you agree we need democracy in the workplace? If yes, what would it look like in your organization? If not, how else would you improve engagement?

10 Look at the Met Opera Dialogue Box in the case study and read the background. How would you have resolved this problem?

04

Dialogue and the digital world

As technology gets smarter, we are getting dumber. Do I have your attention? The fact that technology is everywhere and makes communication so easy means we have to fight to get people's attention, which often involves making blunt, even insulting statements. Whatever your thoughts about the 2016 US election, the shock campaign of candidate Donald J Trump was one for our age. In the 24/7 news cycle, you have to shout to get attention, and you have to get people talking about you. The Trump campaign was a PR campaign based on getting attention controversially, using social media rather than advertising because in the new environment, advertising has a much less influential role than in recent decades. It was in the 2012 election that social media first became a forceful presence. Just as John F Kennedy was the first president for the TV age, Barack Obama became the first president for the social media age. We can see how social online networks influenced the voting in that election. In 2012, 30 per cent of online users said they were urged to vote via social media by family, friends or other social network connections. After voting, 20 per cent of voters actively encouraged others and 22 per cent posted their decision when they voted. It was also financially lucrative because by utilizing social media, the Obama campaign was able to raise close to US $1 billion.

Social media is a tough communications environment. It is often noisy and chaotic. There is not much room for nuance in the digital communication space, and so messages need to be simplified and made powerful to the greatest degree. Digital technology is restructuring the organization or work and business, and in many senses overwhelming individuals in the workplace. The problem is finding a path through the sheer volume of communication, because we are overloaded by the information and messages flying about, and it is difficult to process so many messages in any meaningful way. We need to recognize that the complaints we read about aggression on social media are not just part of a broad social problem; the same dynamics are at work in the organization and we need to figure out how to resolve the problems we have in communication terms. To get attention in this crowded, fast and transient space does not necessarily mean continuously embracing new technologies and hurling more information faster at colleagues and employees. It means figuring out more targeted, experience-based ways of communicating, and defining the focused dialogue you need to have rather than just creating more chatter and more noise. Just as black-and-white photography made a comeback after being crowded out by ubiquitous colour photography, so too should we be looking to the fundamentals of communications and how they can be mixed with technology to create new insights.

In Chapter 1, I highlighted the triangle of internal communications, employee engagement and HR and how they need to see employees as whole persons, not just as numbers or functions. In the crowded digital space we now have, the aim is constantly to understand how these individuals receive and deal with information and engage with the content being communicated. If we take the example of e-mail, we can track that it has been delivered to an address in a database, but has it reached the right person, and if so has it been opened, read, understood, embraced and acted upon? This is what we are trying to achieve with our communications. With the faster and more extensive information flows we witness day in and day out, we are realizing that information flows are turning into a flood of e-mails, messages, attachments, information requests and all kinds of unprocessed data. E-mail has many advantages, but it also shows how work tasks are increasingly fragmented and is a channel that easily panders to compulsive behaviour. E-mail also generates information overload, because it is so easy to do compared to the old days of the typed or handwritten memo. All of which is increasing stress. Which leaves us with the most troubling question in modern communications: how to cope? This is not simply a question of processing large quantities more efficiently in communications terms; it is also a question of how people cope with all this information and the demands on our attention. People's brains literally do not cope with all this information, so they use various strategies and tactics to screen this information rather than engaging with the content. One major strategy to get to individuals is through networks, which in turn gives your receiver a framework or context in which to fit their own struggle.

I've already offered an equation for the communications challenge of managing emotion, so let me suggest three numbers to you: 7, 38 and 55. Exact figures vary according to which experts you read, but I will use the figure of 7 per cent as the figure that represents how much of what we communicate is verbal. There is then 38 per cent vocal communication, which is our tone of voice, inflection and the sounds we make. The remaining 55 per cent is non-verbal, our gestures and other physical body language. As mentioned, figures vary but this is roughly the division of labour when it comes to our communications. Yet, historically, communication has focused on the mere 7 per cent of what is intelligently expressed, and it seems we've been poorly communicating for years, and we are still! Let me suggest another number, and again the expert estimates will vary; the number 30. This refers to the average number of people to whom we will tell an important piece of news. For some people this number will be higher, while lower for others. A great extrovert and natural networker will tell more than 30, while an introvert will tell fewer than 30 or perhaps no one. This obviously grows by a magnitude when translated into people's digital footprint and their personal networks.

In an organization, the challenge is one of finding your natural communicators, those people who have extensive personal networks. Who in your organization can you get a message to so that you reach a greater number? They need not be 'communications people' or important managers; they are simply your natural communicators. This is related to the notion of being interconnected. It is interesting that in our age of heavily networked communications, we are discovering the extent to which we are all networked as people. Thus, communications is not technocratic, which it seemed to be in the 20th century; rather, it is now people-centric. Everyone is a communicator and networker, and communications has to be both a leadership function and a job for everyone. This paradigm shift also indicates that technology is at the service of people, and not the other way around.

Having the tools and networkers to build your online presence and interaction is important, but you need something else; you need engaging content. This is what will build your audience through their networks. In the same way as political campaigns have worked, business organizations and others should be encouraging employees to communicate and encourage communication through their networks. Your employees can be effective advocates for your company and they can be effective activists, either for or against you. If you manage this well then you can encourage activism to support your business, but if you get it wrong then you will find a growing activist community against you. You will find the Dialogue Box is a tool that can help you navigate this problem without having to resort to over-simplification or the insulting and bullying messages so common in social media.

Authority and power in the digital world

Confucius said, 'When the wise man points at the moon the fool looks at the finger.' Technology points to what we can do, and focusing on the channels in internal communications is a way of missing what is truly important. We can have wonderful technology, beautiful-looking images and efficient channels, but all of this needs to point to what you want to achieve. It is content that connects people to your objectives and makes your communication successful. Although we can all get excited by technology, people are also often fearful of it, believing it will do harm or cause problems. Our work is constantly being reinvented in relation to ground-breaking technological innovations, but at the heart of the process are people and their behaviours, and how they respond to change, the subject of the previous chapter. There are many genuine concerns about technology and social media, ranging from robots taking over jobs through to fears that our children are not learning language effectively. As both a threat and an opportunity, we need to be thoughtful about how we use the technologies at our disposal. There are now more than 12 billion connected technology devices in the world, forcing us all to adopt new strategies and rethink the way we do business and what products we need to be offering. It has also led to us redefining our relationships with customers, employees and business partners, as well as our friends, partners and spouses. As noted, the biggest impact in the workplace has been e-mail, but this has created a dependency and set of poor habits that suggest we still have a long way to go in how we make use of the digital power literally at our fingertips.

What technology does give us is greater access to people and events around the world and right next door to us. Technology can help overcome human barriers. It creates more transparency and makes it increasingly hard to hide information, money and actions. It opens up education, allowing for smarter tools to help people learn in their jobs, and even attend or go back to university through distance learning. It also opens up a sense of encounter, and meeting different cultures, races and genders can be made more cooperative when we are familiar with people from diverse backgrounds because first, we understand better and second, we become less fearful or concerned about their differences. However, there are also technological barriers to consider. These are not so much a case of technical barriers per se, more about transforming the way we do things and breaking down resistance to technological change or fear of change. We have our habits and appetites, and technology pushes the limits on these, so we need to push past what we find acceptable and create a new communication space. Our technical abilities are limited by our knowledge; our communication abilities are limited by our imagination and by how far we are able to push ourselves to change and adopt new technology and ways of doing things.

One of the barriers tested is one basic to an organization, and that is the notion of authority. Authority is crucial to how power works in the organization. In the past, we accepted the authority of those people issuing the information from a position of power, and we accepted the edited versions communicated to us through editors and other functionaries. Today, we expect a more open understanding of power and authority; in other words, what has been discussed earlier as democracy in the workplace. Employees can now challenge authority in an organization by putting stories out into the public domain at an extremely low cost. Our laptop or iPhone can be the delivery mechanism to millions, and no one is around to edit us; instead, our editor is popularity. The number of hits, retweets or shares will give it a level of authority. This goes to the extreme that 'post-truth' or fake news can be taken seriously because there are no gatekeepers. Discovering the truth of the matter becomes a public process of discussion, rather than a controlled process prior to publication.

It is, I suggest, no accident that the rampant digitalizing of our social environment, and its challenge to authority and power, has coincided with public debates over the meaning of things and words. One aspect of this is the emergence of power placed in the hands of minority groups, who are now gaining greater access to majority audiences. We should also note that the greater prevalence of impersonal technology has coincided with greater emotionalism in the public space. There is, however, a need for balance between the intelligent and emotional aspects of our lives. An academic colleague of mine summed it up. She was exasperated, she said, by always being told by her students what they feel. She wants to know what they think. In the pursuit of academic excellence and analysis my colleague has a point, because the boundary between intelligence and emotion is, sadly, being eradicated. However, there are many areas of life, including in the workplace, where people want to have their emotions addressed, and rightly so. This makes communication a process of emotional management, and the first step to managing emotions is acknowledgement. In other words, you show them you understand, or are open to understanding, how they are feeling about a situation or their place within any given situation. This is part of the new communication environment we now face. As impersonal technology increases, our emotions and personal experience are also more heightened.

Logic and reasoning are competing with the emotions and feelings of your audience, and sometimes when we attempt to open up a conversation we can find this only creates more emotional storms, rather than a calm debate and an authentic attempt to understand each other. The demand for so-called trigger warnings, advising people that what you say may offend or distress the audience, is part of the problem. Some warnings seem helpful, almost innocuously so, because they help prepare us. Mundane examples have been around a long time, such as ratings for movies advising what age they are suitable for. Professors might want to warn students of offending images or themes, such as the portrayal of race in Mark Twain's *Huckleberry Finn* or flagging discussion of rape cases that may arise in the class. Another aspect of this is what is called micro-aggression, which refers to words or acts that inadvertently offend others, such as asking a British woman who looks Asian, 'Where are you really from?' as it implies she is not truly British. These micro-aggressions are not to be confused with what is downright offensive, such as when a white person blacks their face like a minstrel, thus causing offence to a black person. They are, however, equally offensive to the person on the receiving end, and these boundaries are being pushed much further as societies become more diverse. It is argued that advocating 'being British' or following the 'American Dream' are micro-aggressions, because they assume an historic identity or that opportunity is available to all, rather than perceived bias toward the mostly white portions of British or American society. There is also cultural misappropriation, for example white students holding a Mexican tequila party and dressing up in sombreros, which is seen as stereotyping. Such warnings, though well intentioned, are turning into challenges to free speech in the classroom or the workplace, and can lead to people avoiding hard topics for fear of offending, particularly in respect to race, gender, nationality and religion. However, ultimately these dialogues are focused on power and authority, with minority groups seeking authority for their interests and a role in deployment of power in society. The problem is that when we don't have this dialogue we push the issues deeper underground, and so we should encourage any opportunity to raise awareness and promote good dialogue, and social media is making the issue even more fraught with discord.

Dialogue in the new social space

If we are to have meaningful dialogue in an increasingly angry world, trolled by social media, we need an understanding of why and how we are different, since commonality only goes so deep. We all need to be sensitive to the views and experiences of others, and education and dialogue help us to achieve a better outcome. Education is in part about fostering a degree of robustness in argument, but it also means allowing room for both traditional and progressive voices to be expressed and embraced together, so that we can progress together. The Dialogue Box is a place to explore all these issues, and does so effectively. However, before diving into explaining how the Dialogue Box works, we need to look at the role of digital technology and how it affects our communication environment. The rise and power of technology makes dialogue and effective communication even more critical. We are used to joking about people being on their mobile phones while supposedly doing something together, like having a meal. The joke highlights how people have technology as a barrier between them. We therefore need to create a strategy that combines the best of human interaction and technological facilitation.

The reality of technology is that it is changing faster than we are, which is creating planning and implementation challenges for us all, and since entering the world of communications as a journalist some three decades or so ago I have witnessed this at first hand. Technology makes us feel even more daunted about facing the technological future, but we need to expand our imaginations within the organization to figure out what we need to do in meeting the challenges. Ignoring the pithy warning by Mark Twain that he didn't like to make predictions, especially about the future, I gave a presentation at a conference in London back in 1985, where I offered a peek into the future of finance. I explained how consumer retailers and other top companies (this was before the ubiquitous word 'brand' was all the rage) had reputations and a direct connection with the consumer that would lead to themselves becoming banks. I also discussed how smartcard technology would allow us to combine cards, instead of having to carry the popular 1980s portable Rolodex of credit cards. There was great scepticism about what I was saying, tinged with doubts about my credibility, being a twenty-something journalist. A slightly more humorous occasion, at least for me, was having lunch at the Barclays Bank headquarters dining room in the City. I patiently explained to my host that banks could easily be replaced by Marks & Spencer, Sainsbury's and other retail companies. After all, why do we need the middle man to handle our transaction? After listening patiently to me, my host in turn explained how the reputation and trust of banks was an insurmountable barrier to this happening. I suggested he was assuming people trust banks. Well, we know where that line of thought has ended! The point is, when new technologies emerged in 1980s, as we carried around mobile phones the size of bricks, we were on the brink of a massive sea change in the use of technology in the workplace and at home. There are still more technologies that are evolving which will eventually create new channels for communication. Not only does this impact the business, providing both threats and opportunities for your organization, these technologies will also find their way into the hands of your employees. This means organizations will need to move faster to keep up, and this will require them to either take more risks or establish greater trust with their employees.

Like teenagers challenging parental power, to some extent we are in the adolescent stage of being users of digital technology, because technology itself is still relatively new. We see this adolescence when we see how unhelpful people are when they send e-mails, especially when they use the ubiquitous 'FYI' or send a collection of documents and expect the receiver to know what to do. As the sender, you know why you are sending an e-mail, so take a minute to be clear why you are sending it or what you expect the receiver to do. This will save them time, and if this becomes common practice we will be helping each other in a major way to break down miscommunication and the volume of e-mails, because miscommunication tends to lead to more e-mails seeking clarification or spreading the miscommunication. A helpful way to think of this is to consider how news providers present news and content to you in newspapers or online. They give you the headline which, if it interests you, leads on to you reading the news story. If that is interesting, then you will move on to related stories or in-depth analysis. The content provider guides you through this with headlines and links. This helps some people to go in depth and allows others to decide early how much they want to follow the story. The e-mail subject line is your headline. The body text is your news story, which can use links and sub-headlines to direct your audience in the right way. You can think about managing your own content in this way, which will help you and help your receiver. So, think of yourself as a content provider, because in the 21st century we are all able to be content providers. However, there is a flip side to this ubiquity, because how do we gauge quality, respect and all those other criteria that were once gainfully employed by the mainstream media providers?

Focusing our communication needs on content means looking past the technology and seeing it as an enabler, even a doer, whilst recognizing it is people who create and focus content. Thus, success in social media is not achieved by pushing out lots of information through multiple channels. It is about creating inspiring content that reaches diverse audiences, grabs their attention and meets their needs. Social media is a tool that increases engagement, and it is a wonderful opportunity for companies to engage employees. Yet, they have been reluctant, largely through fear, to be imaginative or push the boundaries. Like the finger pointing at the moon, social media tells us more about the psychology of social behaviours than about the current state of technology. Social media can create a greater sense of empowerment and belonging in a community, and this is the grand prize for any company daring and imaginative enough to harness social media for their employee engagement strategies. The downside is that it is so easy to create an emotional storm that sets people against each other, often driven by the way messages are focused and based on perception, and even fake data.

In Chapter 1, I discussed the notion of infusion. What digital technologies allow is the spread of peer-to-peer dialogue, and this lies at the heart of infusion. Writing in the 1940s and 1950s, the American sociologists Paul Lazarsfeld and Elihu Katz have proposed a two-step model of communication. They explained that people's opinions do not come through direct information from the mass media, but through individual interactions with opinion leaders who are similar in demographics, interests, and socio-economic factors to themselves. Influencers are the people you connect with on your social networks, such as family, friends, colleagues and shared-interest group members. Various levels of trust are created based on these social media relationships and thus drive information and opinions across a variety of open and closed networks. Though their theory has been criticized many times over, it still holds a certain value in explaining the influencing process of social media, though it is rather a more multistep than a simply two-step process. In respect to your employees, the workplace is also such a social space and a network. I have explained that all internal communication is external and vice-versa, and the same applies to these networks; we cannot separate them. This presents us with a challenge in how we manage them.

This also means regularly finding out what matters to them and responding quickly to any concerns or desire for more information or support. The use of employee annual surveys, I respectfully suggest, is a massive waste of time and money. First, it is a snapshot in time and employees change their mind as situations evolve. With the technology we have today, online data collection means you can, indeed you should, be taking the pulse of your employees every second of the day, not every one, two or three years. Digital technology and social networks based on relationships are at the heart of how the workplace is changing, and how it is now radically different from the way we were organized for well over 200 years in the industrial era. These technologies are paving the way to transforming our work and creating new ways of working together. As stated above, we are still at an adolescent stage and we need to reach adulthood in technology in the ways suggested here.

How we will network

5G: A fifth generation of mobile telecommunications is on the way, and likely to become the next single global standard. It will be commonplace during the course of 2017 and will become an economic success story within the next 5 years.

High-altitude stratospheric platforms: These are quasi-stationary aircraft which can deliver networking to a large area while flying at a very high altitude (17–22 km) either in dense urban areas or over a wide geographical area. In other words, they are essentially low-orbit regional communication satellites that combine the advantages of satellites and ground-based systems, giving us a flexible solution to a number of our communications challenges. They will be able to serve a large number of users, and will be great for disaster relief or temporary coverage of entertainment events. They will also become a permanent feature in our communications infrastructure. We are probably about five years away from this starting to happen and it will be around 10 years before it becomes financially viable.

MOOCs: Massive Open Online Courses are online open-access courses aimed at large-scale participation. They can offer unlimited participation, and are revolutionizing the way we approach teaching and learning in universities and corporate education. They are increasingly mainstream today, and while still financially unprofitable they will be fully viable in the next two or three years.

WiGig: Wireless Gigabit will expand Wi-Fi displays in the way wireless networking is developed. WiGig will deliver up to 6 Gbps (6,000 Mbps) connections between devices in internal spaces. We can expect this to become widespread in the next three or four years and an economic success a year or so after that.

Technology and organizing employees

Organizations need to focus on striking a healthy dynamic balance between the human and digital technology elements. Digital technologies give us more collaborative ways of operating, which is what I mean by adulthood instead of the playful attitude of children or the angst-ridden distraction of adolescence. In the last chapter I discussed democracy in the workplace, and we can build on this approach by seeing technology as an enabler for propagating this idea. There are now many studies into the effects of social networking sites (SNS) on offline behaviour, and they demonstrate an active relationship between SNS use and various forms of civic or political engagement, as well as greater levels of participation by youth populations. People who are active in social media also tend to be active in social and political issues, which can either be harnessed to help you or create problems for you. These social networks are used most powerfully not through casual encounters but through a solid relationship network supported by social media. With the emergence of new digital technologies and changes in how work is organized, there are increasing expectations of responsibility, autonomy and ambition at work. This is because of greater transparency and awareness, as well as higher levels of education and training. Digital technologies have opened up the social and emotional aspects of the workplace, which challenges the alienation of the past and highlights a sense of identity, meaning and recognition in the workplace.

How we interface

Annotated-reality glasses: Similar to Google's Glass project, these are glasses you can wear as computers which can mediate the information and ideas between the wearer and the wearer's environment in an intensely intimate and personal way. They are designed to connect the wearer to his/her environment through the mediation of online interfaces, the internet, web, AR information and through personal connectivity to others where possible. Wearable computers can also work off autonomous social networks and servers, rather than using commercial cloud technologies which are designed for surveillance and data storage. Wearable computers can be customized to fit the needs of the groups or persons that use them. They allow contextual information to be overlaid on the user's field of vision. These glasses will become mainstream within the next couple of years and will become commercially successful very quickly.

Context-aware computing: We've all read the stories of people getting stuck on railway tracks or in a field because of SatNav. This is because the technology is limited by the data input and of course the person using it! We cannot slavishly follow the technology, we have to partner with it. This relationship will involve context-aware computing, because the computers will be able to sense and react to their environment. Devices will have information about the circumstances under which they operate, and use rules-based and sensor inputs to respond to the environment accordingly. The intelligence will be enhanced by such devices learning assumptions about the user's current situation and building them into future decisions. Such tools will be available to us commercially within the next 10 years.

Immersive multi-user VR: A fully immersive Virtual Reality environment to which the user connects through direct brain stimulation. All senses would be stimulated, diffusing the boundary between reality and fiction. This presents technical challenges of immersing multiple persons into a single virtual environment, raising many questions about how such joint action behaviour and coordination can become a stable process, a single framework in which several humans can interact, communicate and cooperate in a highly immersive virtual environment. It must account for the social nature of perception and real-time human interaction. Participants can interact with the world and with others from an egocentric perspective by using their physical body as an interaction device. We are a decade away from this technology being more accessible and commercially available.

Telepresence: Remember *Star Wars*? Telepresence is a technology that gives you the sense of being present, through telerobotics, at another location. This can enhance the face-to-face value of making calls through Skype or other video technologies. It will create a telepresence environment that will merge with virtual worlds, resulting in a robust hybrid system that can support avatars, mobile media, simulated environments, and other technology-based reality. For example, students in criminology could join detectives at crime scenes without risking contamination of the crime scene area. This technology is about seven or eight years away and could be commercially viable in a decade's time.

Wall-sized screens: Tile-able and interactive screen wallpapers are expected to dominate all types of surfaces for use in both domestic and professional environments. Wrap-around screens offer enhanced peripheral vision and this creates a deeply immersive viewing experience. Such technology is already available, but will become more common in the next few years and commercially viable well within the next decade.

There have been some negatives around the use of technology in the workplace. The fear of social media in many companies has led them to be cautious in making use of it, with many bans being applied to try to avoid its use internally. New tools have tended to complement existing tools rather than replace them. This creates what some authors call the 'millefeuille effect' because the result is having communication tools pile on top of one another without really forming a single integrated system. Digital technologies have acted as an inhibitor as well, by creating more kinds of reporting, controls, compliance and surveillance. This control makes employees feel constrained and thus creates an increasing sense of alienation from the work, with employees feeling they cannot really express their personality in the workplace. This is the problem of how to empower employees in the adult digital age.

Overloaded? Dealing with the digital volume

Internet of Things

The Internet of Things is a way of explaining how we are connected through any device with an on and off switch to the internet and each other in a relationship between people–people people–things and things–things. The Internet of Things revolves around increased machine-to-machine communication; it's built on cloud computing and networks of data-gathering sensors, and is mobile, virtual, and instantaneous. By 2020 there will be over 26 billion connected devices, an incredible number of connections. Thus, anything that can be connected will be connected, with a variety of devices talking to each other. On a journey to a meeting, you can choose transport and routes given to you by things, and the people you are meeting can be updated on your progress by things. In a larger context, you can be connected to transportation networks in 'smart cities', where we will trigger sensors that control the traffic network and which can help us reduce our environmental impact.

The use of big data

Big data refers to the gathering and storage of large amounts of information for eventual analysis. In the early 2000s, industry analyst Doug Laney defined data in terms of three Vs:

✦ **Volume**: Organizations collect data from a variety of sources, including business transactions, social media and information from sensor or machine-to-machine data, and with new technologies like Hadoop, this becomes easier.

✦ **Velocity**: Data streams flow at an unprecedented speed and need to be managed in a timely manner. RFID tags, sensors and smart metering are driving the need to deal with huge volumes of data as close to real time as possible.

✦ **Variety**: Data comes in various formats, including structured, numeric data in traditional databases, unstructured text documents, e-mail, video, audio, stock ticker data and financial transactions.

Big data can help us look for patterns more powerfully, looking for peaks or troughs in data and what trends are emerging in the data. We can also examine complex data more closely and detect relationships between events, variables and linkages in order to interpret the meaning of data. Big data is important because of what we can do with it and the speed with which we can understand large volumes of data, and take action to address problems and failures, or take decisions and offer new solutions.

There is a generational dimension to this change, as the younger generations are more conditioned by the technology. This, however, is not as simple as it appears at first blush. Young people are not simply a homogeneous group who simply adapt to new technology and always push to introduce companies to new practices. The digital skills of young people are often over-stated. Yes, they can be early adopters and users, but *how* are they adopting and using the technology? Are they slavish in their use or innovative? In the workplace and in the digital world, younger generations constantly seek experience, not a stairway to corporate heaven. Compared to our predecessors, the younger generations are seeking to negotiate a shorter-term experience with their employers. They want quicker returns for the investments they feel they make to the organization; quite a change to the 'alienation' of the 20th-century worker discussed in the last chapter! This generational change impacts how conventional organizational structure and so career 'paths' have changed to be more like 'lily pads' as employees, especially younger ones, look to hop from one experience to another to find their career fulfilment. Open learning environments and distance working are among the new patterns of addressing this. Employees may spend a shorter time in an organization, and then seek new experiences, only to return to your organization later. This means building an HR approach and network which includes staying in touch with former employees and co-workers. Organizations need to accept radically different operational methods from the past, and change has become the new normal, so we cannot promise a return to times when things were seemingly settled. This creates great psychological stress on the workforce as they need to live with uncertainty as a daily state of mind, not a temporary state as a specific change is made.

Conclusion

We are all technologically savvy at one level, but the technology is still too much driven by trivialities and distractions more than work and purpose. Are we using our technology mostly to create involvement in the social, economic and political environment, or is it mainly used as a distraction? We have this wonderful enabling technology, but how do we get from this impersonal technology to personal dialogue, because often the technology is a barrier to good communication and, especially in areas like e-mail use in organizations, it promotes bad behaviours. I started out as a theatre writer and turned into a technology journalist – don't ask! The theatre gave me an enduring interest in dialogue; the technology gave me a grounding in technical matters, their limits and possibilities. I believe we can strike a balance between human dialogue and digital technologies, and the many new developments in the pipeline will help us achieve this, so long as we look at the creative moon and not the technological finger pointing towards what is possible, not fully able to achieve our dreams.

Questions

1 What kind of social media policy does your organization have? Does it set rules or promote good behaviours? Is it creative? How can it be improved to meet some of the challenges raised in this chapter?

2 In the management of new graduates and young employees, what do you see as their digital behaviours? They may be comfortable with technology, but how do they use it? How do you rate their sophistication in relation to the workplace, as opposed to their social or entertainment use?

3 I have highlighted a number of new technologies; how can you incorporate them into your organization in terms of communication? How far are you prepared to look into the future of your digital organization?

4 If you look at your organizational structure, how well do you think it matches the demands of the new digital environment and the mindset of the younger generations?

5 I raise the issues of bullying, abuse and sensitivity towards cultural and other differences. How would you assess your own organization in terms of diversity and how this diversity is managed?

6 How would you define the role and functioning of power and authority within your organization, and what changes do you think are required to create a democracy at work?

7 Do you agree with the idea of democracy at work? If not, why not? If yes, how would you promote the idea internally? Would your leadership accept this idea?

05

Zone 1: Intelligence – how organizations and people think

The great German writer Goethe said that to act is easy; to think is hard. Organizations do a lot of thinking, from product design through to creating their strategy. In communications, it is the thinking component that communications work mostly focuses on: getting the strategy right, writing the media release, crafting the presentation, and other intelligent tasks. This is why it is Zone 1 of the Dialogue Box (see Figure 5.1 on page 116). However, I want to extend this thinking process in the Dialogue Box, to connect thinking to connect employees emotionally. The idea, the words to explain the idea, the strategy to connect – all of these actions involve crafting the right message and understanding the audience. This is important work, but all too often the thinking stops when this work is done, when in fact this is only the beginning. This chapter will address how to understand and build the intelligence in the Dialogue Box for a more thoughtful and connecting way of communicating.

So, what is intelligence?

At its simplest, intelligence is our capacity to be rational and pursue a path of reasoning to reach a decision or conclusion about something. It allows us to discern what we can know and understand why something might be unknown. Having intelligence means we have a capacity for knowledge, and that we are able to take what we know and use our reasoning to systematize it in order to make sense of the data we have before us. It is also our capacity to be objective, to step outside of ourselves and see situations and events from a bird's-eye view and make decisions that affect us and others; we are able self-consciously to think of ourselves as part of this whole process. Another crucial element of intelligence is our capacity to act ethically, and to make decisions on the basis of what is good, which may not necessarily be what we want to do but what we believe is the right thing to do; which is not to say we will do what we should, however intelligent we are! We do not do this in isolation – there is both individual and group intelligence. This means that as individuals we can have intelligence and do all these things I have defined as intelligence, but it also means that as a group of people we can create intelligence and do all these things on a group basis, interdependently or in a supportive manner. All of these aspects can be the focus of our attention, and one aspect may sometimes take precedence over another in vying for our attention. However, there are some significant drawbacks to the intelligent process of rationality and reasoning, not least of all the fact that emotions and our subconscious influence the process, which is precisely what the Dialogue Box identifies as necessary to achieve overall success in our communication.

There are many barriers to reaching intelligent conclusions, and one problem for intelligence is that the discernment of what is or can be known can be eclipsed by the unknowns, the things we don't know, cannot know or are only revealed to us by later information or events. In our reasoning process we may suffer, or struggle, with insufficient knowledge. We also have certain biases and make certain assumptions. We try to fill in the gaps, and in so doing our attention can be steered in the wrong direction, or our eyes fall on the wrong element and our decision or viewpoint is thus faulty. There are occasions when we are unable to systematize to make sense, and hence we need to fill in the gaps based upon assumptions or by seeking out new information. In such moments we may well hold tentative or temporary notions of the complete picture and revise accordingly. There are occasions when we have a diminished capacity to be objective, and our intelligence is usurped by emotions or biases leading to a triumph of a subjective over an objective view. In such circumstances we ignore the facts that do not fit and over-value the facts that do fit to bolster our subjective case. There are occasions when we are challenged by the understood ethical norms, and intelligence allows us to still make use of these norms or rules of thumb to achieve an equitable result. There are occasions when our intelligence is unable to appraise events fully for a number of reasons, which may be because there are key events not occurring that we would expect or had been told would be a precursor to the troubling event. It may be that key information we would expect is not established. Another reason may be that we are struggling with our approach to an event or information because the way is not adequately prepared or because we have been kept in the dark. Hence in a meeting it is good when people are fully introduced, rather than being left to try to figure who an individual is, thereby being distracted from the task of engaging with them. So many occasions where we may fail to have accurate intelligence!

Ordinarily, when a company or organization makes a decision there is much intelligence at work involving many intelligent individuals in the process. There may be many hours, weeks, months and more put into reaching the decision. The decision will have been well researched, discussed in many committees, focus groups and with multiple internal and external parties. Many presentations will have been made, and feedback built into making the decision more robust. So far, so good. Why then is all this intelligent work undermined in the blink of an eye? The answer is emotion, which we will explore in the next chapter. If you recall my example of the company closing down a facility in Chapter 2, this will be used as our example here. Like many major decisions, let's assume this move is announced to the outside media, perhaps at a media conference or in a media release with various specific interviews. In this context, we can only admire the intelligence of the decision or plan, assuming the media portrays the decision in a sympathetic way. The media will ask questions, probe and discuss the decision or plan in a remote sense. Their objective is to see what the story is for them, asking if this is a valid approach, does it have great impact on the local community, will it send the share price up, will it lead to job losses, save the company or draw the wrath of politicians? In other words, is it newsworthy? Any number of news stories or narratives may emerge, depending on the size of the organization, the nature of the decision and its interest to the outside world. The deciding question is simple: does the media narrative match the desired narrative?

The narrative battle you fight is that the decision or plan has its own narrative, the one the company or organization has based its own thinking on in order to reach the decision and the trajectory that is foreseen by the decision-makers. The media conference seeks to get that narrative reflected in what appears in the newspapers, on television and online, but the media will have their own ways of testing the decision and as a result form a different narrative. Media specialists internally and external consultants help to craft the message and materials in order to sell the organization's narrative, or at least to get the reported narrative as close as possible to the organization's narrative. Whatever the outcome, the media reporters are approaching the decision or plan intellectually. They don't really have any emotion vested, except in getting a story or being motivated by a big story or smelling a rat. The question is, are they convinced by the message and narrative they've been presented with and will they more or less report the desired narrative? Hold this thought – we will return to it in the next chapter. The point to take on board here is that the work done on the decision or plan has been based on intelligence and it has been announced with this intelligence to an objective audience. We can admit that there has been some emotion that has gone into the planning, but again we'll hold that thought until the next chapter.

Let us stick with understanding intelligence in the organization and the way decisions are made. When I speak of intelligence I mean it in many ways, not merely as something intellectual or deep thinking. Intelligence is a much bigger word than this, which may explain why people get scared by the word. We should not be scared, because we all have intelligence. As human beings we have this amazing thing called the brain that makes us more self-conscious than other species on our planet, and also makes us more concerned about our future and how we plan for it, aside from the purely instinctive. Animals act with instinct and will make their moves accordingly, but this is all in a short timeframe. An animal being chased will run for cover, but plans little beyond that. Each day an animal plans its movements according to light and dark, the need for food, and such like. Human beings look beyond short timeframes and basic needs. We plan our individual lives up to retirement and death, and we organize our societies for this generation and the generations yet to come.

We are also creative, spiritual and thoughtful. As human beings, we are not hardwired but our brains are wired in a particular way. Our brains are governed by the ability of neurons to forge new connections, to blaze new paths through the cortex, even to assume new roles. We can rewire our brain, and consciously develop our intelligence to learn new things. Our brains do a lot more than those of other species, and we have the capacity to rationalize about ourselves and our situation. We are also conscious of our end, and seek spiritual paths to address our current existence and ideas of what lies beyond this life. We are, in other words, complex intelligent beings. While we often refer to what a rational and reasonable person would do in a situation, thinking through all the angles of a problem, we cannot get the full picture if we exclude the elements in the other zones we will discuss. But even in this zone, intelligence is not simply what is rational. In intelligence we use a lot of educated guesswork and rules of thumb. The brain also has the subconscious, which contains a lot that we, as the name obviously suggests, are not always aware of. When we calculate distance, for instance, we are subconsciously using a range of mathematical data and equations to make a judgement about when to apply the brake on a car or position ourselves to catch a ball in flight. Our brain has this built into it, and we barely pay attention to the fact we can do this and do undertake a lot of work in the brain that goes without us slavishly rationalizing step by step.

However, we also have to recognize that our minds are limited. Each of us, to varying degrees, has limited knowledge, intelligence and attention spans. These are tested when faced with choice and change. Despite the widely held belief that more is better, in other words lots of choice reflects our independence and individuality, in fact the human mind can only cope with so many choices at one particular time. Often for the brain it is less that is more. Offering employees more choice does not necessarily make them feel more empowered or better rewarded. Likewise, we are creatures of habit, some more than others. Offering 'exciting change' is not necessarily enticing or even acceptable to employees. Among the most controversial decisions a CEO or leader can make is to change the work schedule or workspace of an employee. We think we always have to think 'outside of the box' but the brain often wants to live inside the box, and assesses situations and data to fit within a box. It is easier to analyse three choices than thirty. Faced with an overwhelming choice, we in fact tend to resort to familiar choices, things we heard of, or just plain make a lazy decision. We then fall into habitual practices. Even choosing the familiar is often an extension of lazy thinking. I say this not to insult or lay blame, after all we all do this at some level. Some of us may love to analyse and offer a fantasy league World Soccer XI line-up involving a lot of choices and analysis of choices, but prefer to choose one soap powder over another because of habit or familiarity.

In making choices our brains exclude data, trying to strip away the extraneous to get at the essential. However, in this process our level of knowledge, assumptions and other factors come into play in excluding things, sometimes to the detriment of a good decision, which might explain why so many bad decisions are taken! Making choices is about making sense of a variety of data points and what we see before us. We have documents and reports, we meet people and influencers, and we have a range of assumptions and a sense of the trajectory for these assumptions, all of which combine to make a decision and all of the time involve us in seeking to make sense. It is not simply that we have all the data and just need to make sense of it; quite the reverse is often the case, because data is missing. The eye is a camera, with a lens that makes sense of data. This extends to how we approach situations that at first don't seem to make sense. We fill in the missing pieces and try to complete the incomplete picture we are presented with. Again, we do not do this entirely rationally; we are influenced by a variety of factors. In an organization we are surrounded by influencers – people who can have a say on what we think. The right, or wrong, thing said at the wrong, right, time can have enormous impact, because it may cause us to fill in a gap we see and forms the basis of what we decide we know about a person or situation. It may not, however, be the missing piece. In the politics of an organization, this is where vulnerability creeps in, as rationality yields to perception. In understanding perception, we see that knowledge becomes negotiable.

The power of knowledge

Knowledge is power, we've all heard that. It leads managers to hold on to information as a power play. It can be used at critical points to influence a decision. Organizational gatekeepers will guard knowledge or information to maintain their authority or control over a person or situation. Their possession of knowledge makes them attractive, and it seduces people into a particular power relationship with them. Here's the thing. Francis Bacon wrote that money should be like manure, effective only when spread about. Information and knowledge are the same. If knowledge is shared then it can produce teamwork and results, spread like manure to grow a nice crop of success. If it is hoarded like manure in a barn, it will soon begin to stink. How smelly is your organization? This is a seemingly silly question to ask, but I've asked it and you should be able to answer it.

Another thing about knowledge is that it is frequently observed we live in a knowledge economy. The role and importance of knowledge are frequently talked about, as if it were purely something objective to be captured, stored and used. I contend knowledge is much more dynamic than this, because it is much more nebulous than this common picture implies. It is perhaps not surprising then that most organizations struggle with knowledge management. This is not a book on knowledge management, but there are some important aspects of knowledge that are relevant to discuss here. Knowledge is part of intelligence, since it impacts how we think. In situations of low knowledge we are in learning phases, and more reliant upon external resources and consultants to create knowledge within the organization. The more we know then the more we can create and innovate new products, services and, of course, knowledge. This all contributes to the organization's knowledge capital, and the ability of your organization to be a learning organization.

A key reason for knowledge being difficult to grapple with is the speed of change. What we know is changing all the time, and we are constantly creating new knowledge and making old knowledge redundant. We can start a major project and quickly find ourselves in a race against redundancy. On one level we love technology, and all the possibilities of finding knowledge that it opens up to us. I have to confess that doing my PhD was so much easier with modern technology, to the extent I find it hard to imagine how people used to do PhDs with pen or typewriter. I could edit and rewrite more quickly. I could access research all over the world, and consult texts, journals, reports and other research sources from my own computer, rather than having to travel to the source. In this respect, the role of technology is welcomed as an enabler.

However, it is also, as already suggested, a threat. There is a constant need to capture know-how and develop the acquisition of skills, which creates a real need for employees to change. Yet, many employees do not readily welcome change. Remember, we are creatures of habit, and for many having to change the way we do things is disruptive to our work and behaviour patterns. The CEO may make change sound like exciting and challenging stuff, but the reality is that many of your employees do not want excitement and challenge; they just want a job, pay and an ordered life. Technological change threatens that order, creating the need to change habits and our approach to work. We know that technology is making knowledge more and more commodified, and this makes it more mundane and more easily accessible, but it also reveals that there is just so much of it and it is harder to discern the authority of knowledge. Just look at Wikipedia. Another aspect of this change in knowledge is that it is increasingly codified for ease of access across the organization, which becomes the source of authority. The organization sets what it believes to be a code of business practice, ethics and other forms of knowledge that are, on closer inspection, more highly contestable than the code suggests. A final aspect to mention is that the need to simplify information can breed indifference and cynicism or it can inspire and motivate. The difference lies in whether our communication is 'dumbing down' or making information intelligent but digestible. Do we befuddle or do we enlighten? This is at the heart of how we get an employee's attention, and whether we manage our communications for the right or wrong reasons.

Getting your employees' attention

One day I was waiting for the train on the London Underground. As the train drew into the platform I noticed a woman eating a burger in the carriage that came to a stop in front of me, and decided to choose the next carriage, since I have a dislike for the odour of other people's hot food in enclosed spaces. I sat down and the train carried on its way to the next station, where a man boarded and sat beside me with a gross-looking meat pie or pasty, which I glanced at. I debated with myself whether to change seats, or accept that in avoiding the burger woman I was stuck with the meat pie guy, when someone opposite said: 'Oi, you're the guy on the telly.' I looked at Mr Meat Pie next to me only to discover it was the actor Damian Lewis, at the time famous for his role in *Homeland*. As an aside, I had been looking at the DVD set of Series 1 that very morning, as my wife had asked me to buy the series, though I wasn't sure. I asked him if he enjoyed doing the series, which he did, so I decided to buy it after all. Anyway, the point of the story is how my attention was focused. My focus had been in a sense set by the experience of avoiding Mrs Burger, so when a man sits next to me I am focused on Mr Meat Pie rather than Mr Famous Actor. My attention was then refocused when I overheard someone say: 'Oi, you're the guy on the telly.' My brain was excluding certain data and focusing on other data, excluding identification of the man and focusing on the pie.

In an organization, given the constant flux of change and the level of innate resistance to it, how are we then to get the attention of our employees? How are we going to say: 'Oi, you're the guy on the telly?' In addition, why is it their attention we need? Let's answer the second point first; it's the easiest. I am equating attention here with engagement. To have an engaged workforce is not about creating happiness for employees or beating the drum; it is about getting their attention and focus at work, which will increase productivity. That's the easy answer. The more difficult part is to answer how we get their attention in the first place, and how we ensure we get lasting attention. The reason it is more difficult is that getting the attention of an employee's mental real estate is a great challenge. They have other priorities, and may not have as much love for the organization they work for as you do – perhaps they have less invested in their work or position. Great profit figures tend to get the attention of senior managers with stock options to calculate, but may be of less interest to a shop-floor worker on minimum wage; quite reasonably, as they do not perceive the direct benefits, even though the financial strength of the company is what pays their wage. Getting employees' attention is not just a question of hierarchy though. When it comes to talent retention, for instance, we want to harness people's talent and their ambition. We want them to see a future in the organization, and for them to see their job or career can expand or flourish by staying. We want to get their attention focused on ambition. However, if we think about ambition, there are ambitious people on the shop floor of a manufacturing plant or in the post room. Equally, there is a lack of ambition to be found in the comfortable life of a middle manager, happily biding their time, bereft of ambition. Whether we are talking careers and ambition, or new policies or facilities developed by HR, how you get attention is by understanding the types of people in your organization, not the level they are at. News of a crèche can equally excite a parent in the accounts department as it will the parent working at reception.

What we want to do is understand the employee and their wants, without being too intrusive or disingenuous. Employees don't necessarily want us to know more, or to get too close. Many employees are only too happy if they never meet the CEO, or only have an arm's-length relationship with their boss. This means we have to employ different strategies to engage different employees, with no single solution or silver bullet. Equally in team-building, some people want to maintain a distance that may not fit in with popular conceptions of 'team', and there is nothing wrong in this. In employee relationships, trying to learn too much about each other may be counterproductive. Some people work better by having a certain level of independence or control. The key is not to have 'happiness' exercises; it is to have an understanding of what makes the people we have responsibility for tick, and to respect their personalities so long as it is not causing a problem for the unit or team. Intelligent management means having the intelligence to see and interpret people's behaviour, engage with the other person's point of view and understanding how they focus on their work.

When it comes to focus on work, one of the myths of the modern workplace is the idea of multitasking. We do not really multitask. We simply divert our attention to several tasks, at best being something like a 'jack of all trades' and at worse losing focus on the chief task that stands before us. The only true workplace multitasking is the organization of teams or units to do set tasks in parallel. Different people focus differently; in other words they are attentive to different things within the workplace, which sorts out who can do general

The multitask myth

'There is time enough for everything in the course of the day, if you do but one thing at once, but there is not time enough in the year, if you will do two things at a time.' (Lord Chesterfield in a letter to his son in the 1740s)

Everybody hears about multitasking all the time, people are always talking about it and there's always that little joke about women being able to multitask while men can't, or women being better at it than men. So what is multitasking exactly? Multitasking, as the name suggests, is doing more than one task at any given time. It can also mean alternating between different tasks or rapidly completing tasks one after another. Some examples of multitasking we do every day include: replying to e-mails and listening to music while sipping your coffee or tea in the morning, having a conversation over a meal, texting and walking; these are all pretty basic examples but you get the point. So yes, we do multitask, but are we good at it? Well, not really. There have been a multitude of studies on this area, most of which have come to the conclusion that multitasking isn't actually all that efficient after all. When we multitask it actually takes longer to complete these tasks, because we make more mistakes and we take more time recognizing new occurrences. Multitasking can also hinder our learning process, since the rate of retention for learning new things is actually lowered when we are multitasking.

And to put an end to the famous multitasking myth about women, a study published in 2013 by Timo Mantyla of Stockholm University suggests that women are worse at multitasking during a certain point in their menstrual cycle, but at other times men and women are pretty much equal in their ability to multitask.

tasks and who can do detailed tasks. Some people respond well to visual stimulus, while others respond more to oral stimulus. Some people like to hear stories to explain a situation, while others want it plain and simple in a set of instructions. This is part of intelligence and attention, understanding how each person focuses and what they need to focus on, and then how to get a point or a need across in a way easily grasped or attended to by employees. There will not be a one-size-fits-all approach, so a communications mix is needed that will hit different audiences at different times and in different ways. This is a far cry from the old broadcast method of communication.

We want receipt of instructions and response by the receiver, not just delivery of information. This is what engagement means – it means getting attention and getting the desired response.

This means we need to have a better understanding of how people think, and we need to learn a lot more about how our employees' brains work, key to which is attentiveness. The importance of attention is that it helps us to corral our ideas, knowledge and emotions. If we can get employees to give their attention to certain things then we will be supporting them to corral their ideas, their knowledge and their emotions to match with the needs of the organization. This is how we can best engage them. In times of negativity for individuals and employees this means trying to divert from the negative with a focus on the positive, replacing one focus with another. Each of us has a hard time at work, our off days, and each organization goes through rough patches. During these times we burn up a lot of energy and goodwill, but we can recapture it by leading people towards a better horizon, a better sense of where they are going and where the organization is going. To do this authentically means you need to be realistic about where they, you and the organization are in relation to that horizon. The problem so often is that leaders and their communications are too remote from the horizon they set, and do not acknowledge this, and so they are set to fail.

Such an approach and acknowledgement means understanding the true role of organizational values, because our values will determine actions. They will underpin the authenticity of the approach and the attainability of the horizon you are directing attention towards. I mentioned that people often focus on the negative, but attending to the negative can be offset by our desire for positive experience. People may gravitate towards the negative, but they do have a real desire for the positive; it's just harder to harness. It is a behavioural issue, and it demands understanding a little more about how the brain works. Research into neuroplasticity demonstrates that what we pay attention to changes our brain, and this in turn changes our behaviour. The implication is that just as we exercise our bodies we can exercise our minds to create behavioural change. Now, we commonly hear of left and right brain activity which, while often talked about, is only a partial picture. The full picture is that the more complex the activity we are using our brain for the more there is a combining of left and right brain to create a solution. It is a balancing act our brains do to achieve a result.

As I said, we have a desire for the positive, and so if we foreground the positive we help to expand attention and focus. Furthermore, if we take a positive approach to others in an engaging way this leads to greater activity by the individual. The brain, when left to its own devices, tends to become introspective and less productive, but when its attention is towards others and activities then it becomes more positive. This is how we can exercise the brain in the work-place, and explains why teamwork is important and productive. In assessing this need, we ought also to recognize those whose work is more individual or remote. Just as an individual can be alone in a far-flung field office, an individual can be quite alone in an assembly line doing repetitive tasks and letting their brain wander. We can find ways to exercise the brain through communications, to keep the attention needed to support the overall goals of the organiza-tion. As well as exercise, the brain needs appropriate rest. Hence tiredness, and the machismo of working late hours in a corporate 'pissing contest', is counterproductive. Resting the brain can give it a good break, which can also be achieved by turning attention to something else. These approaches will help the brain come back fresh to the task at hand, rather than a relentless focus on the same problem or task.

Placing our attention on others helps us to connect to others, which is why role models and individual stories can help connect employees. There are many ways to inspire new horizons and direct attention towards organizational goals through good internal communica-tion. In communicating to employees you can show them the cus-tomer making use of their work or how it fits into a larger context or project. It's like the oft-quoted, though I suspect apocryphal, story of the president visiting Cape Canaveral and asking a guy sweeping the floors what he did, to which the sweeper replied, 'I help put men on the moon.' The moral of the story is the pride the sweeper took in the small part he played in the incredible achievement of put-ting the first men on the moon. One may wonder why a president needs to ask the question, but the inspiring point remains valid. In fact, it seems to draw on an earlier moral tale of Sir Christopher

Wren, architect of St Paul's Cathedral in London and the Sheldonian Theatre in Oxford referred to in Chapter 2, who walked one day incognito among workers during the building of the Cathedral and asked one of them, 'What are you doing?' The man replied, 'I am cutting a piece of stone.' He asked another, who answered, 'I am earning five shillings twopence a day.' To a third man he asked, the answer came back, 'I am helping Sir Christopher Wren build a beautiful cathedral.' This third man had vision, looking beyond the cutting of the stone and his daily wage to the creation of a work of art, a great cathedral that is so much a feature of London's skyline. This man's work remains in our imagination even today, whatever his small role may have been. There are different versions of the story, and in all likelihood there was someone telling this story during the building of the pyramids. However, whatever the story we tell, the point is the same – that the task someone undertakes in an organization is an enabling task in a bigger picture of what the organization is achieving.

The fundamental point to grasp here is that your employees are individuals who seek self-worth just as much as the next person. Their work is important to them, even if they don't like it, simply by virtue of taking up so many hours of their day and determining what sort of life they have at home. While you do not want to intrude on the home in your communications, you need to balance this with the fact that the home context can be affirmative in the employee view of the workplace. It is important to make this connection, but in a respectful way. While we are all keen to go all-electronic, internal magazines play a role in this affirmation process, because employees can take it home and show it to their loved ones and families, so they can see the employee or friends at work being recognized. Electronic magazines do not achieve this so readily, especially since many employees will leave work without wanting to open an electronic gateway to their workplace, but they would consider taking home the 'company rag'. Another approach is to invite families to the workplace for visits, or hold a 'family day' to thank families and close friends of employees. These approaches are not simply 'good PR', they are your company values at work. Recognition of work and support should include families, who can be supportive to employees when times or personal work issues are tough. This is what it means to be a caring organization, and to be a community.

The intelligent organization: Consensus and learning

A PA of mine many years back presented me with a cartoon of baboons in a tree, representing corporate life. The caption read: 'Corporate life is like baboons in a tree. The baboons at the top of the tree look down and all they see are smiling faces, while the baboons further down look up and all they see are assholes.' There is some truth to this picture, and it is a cartoon that corporate leaders should look at from time to time as a reality check to remind them there are other views of reality, especially among their employees. A somewhat different (and more encouraging!) way of looking at corporate life is that if someone wants to feel better about themselves then they focus on someone lower down in the organization, but if they want to be inspired they focus on someone in a leadership position. When employees focus on how their work impacts others they gain greater satisfaction; the work they do is not in itself as valuable to them. Showing the end point of the employees' work boosts production, they lift their eyes up to a higher and more inspiring horizon, and it doesn't have to be baboons in the corporate tree!

To set sights on the horizon the intelligent organization has to identify a narrative, which entails seeking to define narratives for all stakeholders, with the strategy being the all-important narrative that attracts customers, employees and investors alike. Curiously, the great business narrators are journalists and yet there are many journalists who make a move into corporate communications but don't manage to make the transition very successfully. Many do make the transition, and there are many great PR and communications people who came out of journalism. It is important to mention this, and helps to explain one of the key issues in corporate communication that we will return to later, and this is narrative. As narrator, the journalist is always out to get 'the story', in other words to craft an objective narrative of all the elements and events and tell the story of what is going on for an audience. The corporate decision-making process also crafts a narrative, the one they want to tell the company and the world outside about decisions and actions they are taking to make the company more successful. In the case of the journalist, this is an objective telling (or ought to be; there are many cases of journalistic bias!). In the case of a company leadership, it is a subjective telling. Unfortunately in this subjective telling of the narrative and sub-narratives there are too many what used to be called 'yes men', who remain a factor in the company decision-making process today. These are people who do not question the narrative set by the leadership; they merely give their assent. A good CEO needs a good challenger, someone who can question the narrative the leadership has set their heart on, because sometimes it is the wrong narrative and the organization is led down the wrong path.

This questioning is important. Certainly it is important that the leadership has a strong vision and believes in what they are doing, but they also have to have room for questioning, which is at the heart of the learning organization. Many companies today have learning centres, their own universities and various education programmes that are helping them to improve as learning organizations. Naturally, education is an important aspect of intelligence. This is not just about going to school or university, but also ongoing learning and learning on-the-job. One of the welcome trends in education is the development of lifelong learning, adult education and different paths to this learning, such as online and distance programmes. However, there is a downside in our schools, where we find there is too much of a cookie-cutter approach to education these days and a system that has less tolerance for people who do not proceed at the pace we expect, and ignores the fact that some people are late developers. What education also does, apart from providing these skills and functional aspects of learning, is to create an organizational brain, which builds knowledge and questions assumptions within the organization.

Do you like your job?

A lot of us have experienced those Monday Blues; the weekend is over and it's time for work again and sometimes we're really not too pleased about it. Work can be quite stressful and not always very enjoyable, especially when we don't actually like what we do. I think we can accept that work is not easy and is not the most fun activity in the world, but it has to be done. That said, there are those lucky few like Beyoncé or a travel writer who have amazing jobs, where they have fun and love what they do. So what about the rest of us – can we love what we do and enjoy work, even though we're not an international pop star or don't travel the world practically for free? Well, yes we can and there are many people who do love their jobs and enjoy working; you just need to pick the right job for your skillset. When we find a job in which we are suited with the correct skills, there is an opportunity for us to grow our skills and we feel challenged. Challenge keeps us motivated and interested in our work – have you ever disliked doing something you're actually interested in?

When playing a game, for instance, there are many levels to challenge and engage the player. They continue to play because they want to master each level and gain rewards, feeling a sense of achievement. If the levels were all the same and the game never got any harder, the player would become bored and just stop playing it because they are no longer challenged; they just end up disliking playing the game. This is a simplified way of looking at why some people enjoy their work and why some people do not.

Aside from this, people who love their jobs have a certain mindset and are highly motivated. They do not lose sight of why they love what they do and when they began to love doing it. They are often passionate and don't let others put them down or talk them out of pursuing their dream job. They also have the ability to realize that they will not always love what they do because you will always have to do some things you do not want to do – they have some perspective.

Interestingly there have been studies showing that the more money you are paid to do a job, the less pleasurable it is for you to do that job. This can be seen with volunteer workers or people working for charities. For instance, the doctors who go to Africa to immunize children (hardly getting paid or not at all!) get a lot more satisfaction than giving flu shots to people back in their surgery at home.

A US study, published in 2016 by the Society for Human Resource Management (SHRM) on employee job satisfaction and engagement, showed 88 per cent of US employees reported overall satisfaction with their current job. The report also found that 37 per cent reported they were very satisfied and 51 per cent that they were somewhat satisfied. This percentage marks the highest level of satisfaction over the last 10 years, with overall satisfaction up from a low of 77 per cent found in their 2005 study.

Building the learning organization

While nearly everyone complains about having to go to work, especially at the start of the working week, the truth is that people largely enjoy being at work, and it is important to them as we've seen. What employees need is to stretch a little at work, to avoid the repetitive. It is easy to get bored and to lose focus with the repetitive and mundane, to lose attention as discussed. The learning organization is one that keeps pace with the changing circumstances of their workforce, and finds ways to stimulate in an engaging way. We have seen that attention is key to human behaviour, which is about focus rather than skill or ability. However, an attentive workforce is a learning workforce. To engage and get employees' attention the common wisdom is that we have to survey employee attitudes, and so it is commonplace for companies to do employee surveys and other testing on a regular basis. However, I venture to suggest these are not really that useful. Firstly, many of the most inconvenient findings go largely unconfronted, except at a very superficial level. If they were taken seriously then internal communications and human resources would be better resourced. Secondly, they are reflective exercises, in the sense that they call on employees to reflect on their experience, which is not as helpful as people think – it is already processed and mediated by memory and subsequent circumstances. Employees will often answer based on their feeling and situation at the time of the survey, not the time when various events were happening; in other words, they are not done in real time. Many of the best results can be achieved by simple polling exercises, done in a more fun way online or on the shop floor, and with considerably less cost and interference. If there is one thing employees frequently say, especially managers, it is that they are surveyed too often by this consultancy or that specialist, often without seeing any visible results at the end. One method that may find itself more influential in the workplace in the future is the Experience Sampling Method (ESM).

ESM, developed by psychologist Mihaly Csikszentmihalyi at Claremont, involves participants wearing a pager or watch that beeps randomly at two-hour points during the course of a set number of weeks. When the beep goes off, the participant writes down key aspects of their situation at that point, such as where they are, the specific act they are doing, who is with them and how they feel about what they are doing, in other words recording emotion in real time. This is instead of filling in questionnaires at a much later point and reflecting on a range of times, places, people and feelings. The technique is some 30 years old, and has produced data that supports the notion that people enjoy their work when they are focused on it and time is quickly passing. This and other research supports the thesis that people are happiest at work when they are so focused that the day flies by, rather than drags on. When you are focused you lose sense of time, and you reflect less on yourself and actions; you cease to narrate and act instead. It is this activity that ESM measures. This understanding draws on the fact that reward comes from the joy of doing, not just the pay or getting awards, though they help! In a low-energy company employees can spend time distracted and bored, alternating with moments of interest in their work or with their colleagues. A high-energy company will have motivated employees, working and learning together. It is unlikely that such a company exists that is high energy all the time; it is more of an average, or may be an average across their employee base. The goal is to keep stimulating employees as much as possible to be as high energy as consistently as possible, which is what an engaged workforce will be. This is not a question of making them happy, so for goodness' sake never ask your employees if they are happy, and never ask an individual employee, 'Are you happy here?' Happiness is a reflection rather than a state of being. We realize we have been made happy by doing things that engaged us and by living in a state of being where we are absorbed by things, not happiness in itself. The real question to ask is 'are you engaged here?'

One way to engage that I've often suggested, and as yet have seen little evidence of it happening, is to get employees to do someone else's job for a day. This idea falls under the category of risk behaviour in a company, and so managers shy away from it. Yet companies take risks a lot, it is inherent in business, but rarely do they take risks with employees. We can learn a lot from doing someone else's tasks, seeing what they see and do, and perhaps this makes us more appreciative of the job we do. As the saying goes, the grass is not always greener on the other side of the fence. Perhaps I'm asking too much here, and it is just too disruptive for organizations to consider, but I would love to hear experiences of this if they exist. There are also low-level ways to achieve engaging results, and this is by finding ways to turn elements of work into a game, such as competitions, polls and quizzes. There are creative and fun ways to engage your employees and to educate them, and to help them grasp the organizational goals. However, this is not one-way traffic. By getting this engagement you can find employees contributing ideas and stories that move the organization along. Employees will volunteer their ideas and stories more readily, from which the leadership can learn new things and directions as well.

The Dialogue Box: Focus on intelligence

FIGURE 5.1 The Dialogue Box: Focus on intelligence

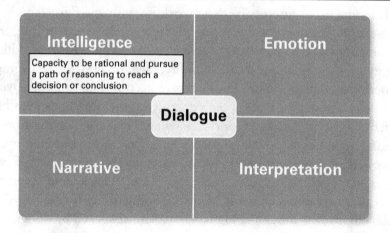

Conclusion

Mark Twain said he didn't like to make predictions, especially about the future. We make decisions about our future all the time. We are narrating a moment, telling stories about ourselves, which do not necessarily match with our reality. This can be either positive or negative. The positive means we are being aspirational, stretching ourselves toward a goal just beyond our reach but motivated in the process. It can be negative, when we set unrealistic goals or goals too far out of our reach. For example, an industrial company that sets a goal of zero accidents for safety is being unrealistic, and lacks credibility for its campaign. We can appreciate the sentiment but it is too easily trumped by the reality. Maybe one day there will not be accidents in industry, and it may one day be a realistic goal, but we are far from this situation today for many industries. It is better to set a safety campaign realistically targeting a percentage decrease in accidents or some other way of illustrating the aim. Your employees are intelligent; they understand the realities. Give them that respect. One aspect that undermines such a safety aim is when pressure is put on managers to reach certain outputs, which leads to the cutting of corners and thus safety issues. The safety campaign has to have an integrity, and intelligent design that balances these realities. The problem is that all too often internal campaigns are 'just PR' campaigns, because they lack this integrity. The intelligent observer will all too often see the contradictions, and there will be serious objections to the narratives set by leadership, leading to a lack of traction within the organization. In using this zone of the Dialogue Box, your task is to set out the bare facts, timelines, milestones and all the other data that is objective and all parties can, or are likely to, accept. In this way, we can exclude some of the emotions and distinguish what is fact from what is interpretation. All too often we argue over 'facts' which are in reality interpretations. This is the important foundational work to be done here so you can take the first steps to effective dialogue.

In making decisions or defining strategy we seek to predict the future, setting in train actions that should have a predictable trajectory and achieve the goal we set out to achieve. Things will often turn out the way we expect, but often, and in the biggest cases, they will not. The process is, on closer inspection, more fraught and less predictable than expected. One reason for this is what is left out of the process, and in our study the core component that is left out or inadequately processed is the employee reaction or engagement. In order to understand this process and improve the employee engagement we need to look at the role of emotion, the second zone in our Dialogue Box.

Questions

1   Is knowledge management a priority in your organization, and how is it managed? What role does communication play in this work? How do you access the knowledge that exists within your organization, both in the sense of getting knowledge out of employees and circulating knowledge around the organization? In what ways might you improve this, and what fundamental approach do you think your organization should take towards knowledge in the 21st century?

2   How much of your communication is a process of deciding at the top and 'cascading' down to employees? Are you innovative or engaging in the ways you get the attention of employees? Do you tend to speak more immediately, readily and openly to the outside world than you do internally?

3   Is there a consensus approach in decision-making? This can be good, in the sense of being collegiate, but it can be bad, in the sense of being 'yes' men and women. Does the communication function challenge the decisions and the way they are managed within the organization? Does the leadership recognize the extent to which they are defining a narrative they expect employees to embrace, without necessarily giving them the support or insight to follow the narrative?

4   Time for a personal question: do you like your job? Think about your job and what parts you enjoy and what you dislike. Look at the jobs of others and think about what they might enjoy or not enjoy. Across the whole employee base, ask the question, 'What's in it for me?' What sorts of answers might people give, and what is your answer?

5   To what extent does your organization do surveys and polling exercises? What sorts of results do you get? How often is your employee survey, and how well is this communicated? Regarding the issues raised by surveys and polls, assess how effectively they are responded to and managed.

06

Zone 2: Emotion – how organizations and people feel

Imagine you have an important meeting to get to, and you must not be late. Maybe it's an important client, a big sales opportunity or a top politician. You have planned what you need to say; you've decided how to get there. Now imagine you've taken the train and the meeting place is a couple of blocks away, and you've built into your planning a bit of fresh air to collect your thoughts and to walk coolly into this important meeting. So far, so good. You're just leaving the station and someone knocks into you and spills coffee on your shoes, not enough to ruin your outfit but enough to really get you annoyed. What happens? There is a good chance you'll challenge this person, complain about how careless they have been, looking for some act of contrition perhaps. What has happened, in fact, is that your emotions have been stirred up, and what is more important is giving this person the benefits of your wrath rather than, well rather than what? Your meeting, remember that? How you were all prepared, how you would clear your head, coolly arrive at the meeting? All the rational and intelligent stuff determined in a cooler time and place. All the plans are out of the window, and your priorities have shifted.

This is an everyday and trite example, but it amply illustrates what happens in an organization as well. You've done all the work: done the research, figured out the strategy, crafted the media release. It's a wonderful plan; it's great news! Then what? Employees hear about the 'great news' from a customer, a competitor, online as they sit bored on the train going to work. This is the single biggest complaint I've heard in many organizations: 'the outside world gets told before we do!' Even great news becomes less exciting, engaging or effective under these conditions. The emotions refocus the employee attention away from where you want it to be. The emotional component is the one all too often ignored in the planning process. The timing of the message or the style in which it is released can be used to boost your message, but it can also set your project or message back. To communicate and engage successfully requires understanding the emotional state of individuals and organizations, and using this understanding to present change and challenges in the most effective way by emotional management. The focus on this zone in the Dialogue Box (see Figure 6.1) will help you to make sure you do not ignore the emotions, but more than this it will help you to harness emotions in your organization positively and thus engage your employees more effectively.

What is emotion?

It is important to understand emotion if we are to understand communication. We live in an age of much more open emotions, for better or worse. The way of being 'businesslike' or communicating on a 'need-to-know' basis is considerably more restricted today, and part of this is because the emotional dimension of human behaviour in organizations is increasingly recognized. People either want or feel entitled to have their emotions in the workplace recognized, which has had the effect of organizations increasingly having to pay attention to the emotional needs of their employees. However, if you think this is all about making employees 'happy' then you would be mistaken, and equally if you believe a 'feel-good' PR campaign will do the trick then again you would be labouring under a false impression. In thinking of emotion, we should not have in mind someone being all emotional, upset or getting angry, although these are aspects. We require a more nuanced understanding of emotion. This means understanding that

FIGURE 6.1 The Dialogue Box: Focus on emotion

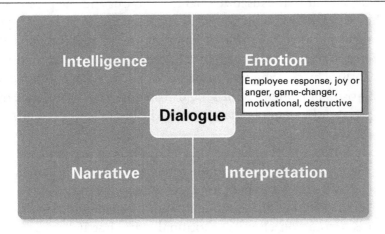

emotion is about mood, motivation and instinct. Emotion is not just 'soft stuff' or feelings. It is also hard stuff because it speaks to how we are motivated and how attuned we are to our instincts. It is not intelligence that spurs our motivation or opens the door to our instincts; it is more a case of the emotions being harnessed, though sometimes almost on a collision course with our intelligence.

When people get emotional, what is happening is that their primary emotions are combined with intelligence to assess a situation. When approaching a situation, we make an intelligent appraisal of it and this combines with a physiological change that spurs action. Let me use an example to illustrate this. You are walking down a quiet street late at night, when suddenly the street lights go off. You see someone lurking in an entrance way to a dark building. What do you do? The first thing you do instinctively is to make an intelligent appraisal, which draws on your existing knowledge. You have the instinct that a dark street is a potential danger, and your intelligence tells you that people lurking in dark entrances can be a danger as well. You may even link this to the event of the lights going off; perhaps someone deliberately broke the lights. This generates a physiological change drawing on fear, which causes the action of evading the situation. You turn around and walk in the opposite direction, perhaps run, look for a passing taxi, whatever gets you away from the danger you perceive, rightly or wrongly. The point to understand in this story is how emotion and intelligence combine to cause an action. If we approached this purely rationally, we might explain that there was a broken circuit that caused the lights to go out and the person was not lurking, but was with someone else in a romantic tryst, saying goodnight. However, the role of emotion and its use of knowledge and perception is a powerful factor. It leads us to create or rearrange our priorities by creating new priorities or rearranging existing ones. These stories of going to a meeting or being in a dark street are trite examples, but I will apply them later to the organizational context.

We see emotions in people every day, but we do more than see – we often react. Emotions are commonly revealed physically, and so we see anger and sadness in people's faces and body language. How do we react? Let's take the example of seeing someone looking bored, which is a common enough emotional state, but in this case it is while we are presenting at a meeting we are in charge of, where we expect nothing but the most rapt and expectant attention! Perhaps we react with anger that they're not listening to us. The question is, what are we really reacting to? There may be a good reason why they are bored, or perhaps what we read as boredom is actually depression or some other emotion. Perhaps the person just looks bored all the time. There are many occasions where emotions are running more deeply and are difficult to read. Good management entails managing both our emotions and the emotions of others. Face-to-face remains still the most effective form of communication, because in this aspect we are able to give the full message, mind and body, to the intended recipient, and can try to read their response, including attempting to read their emotional state.

In Chapter 1, I suggested that communications comes down to the simple equation of: $C = IQ + EQ^{10+}$.

Hence, in communications we are in the job of emotional management. It means trying to raise the emotional pitch when the news is good, and keeping the emotional mood down when the news is bad. In order to do this we need to understand how to read emotions. We can do this on a personal level and an organizational level. Here we will focus on the organizational level. We discussed the primary emotions combining in the example of walking in an unlit street. Let's apply this idea to the organization, specifically in the not uncommon case of a reorganization. In these situations, the primary emotions of uncertainty and loss of colleagues can combine to create fear among employees that there are more job losses or negative changes to come, even if this is not true. This can undermine the morale of a small department or a large organization. When such emotions erupt, there is a physiological change that can cause tiredness or restlessness in employees, resulting in various actions such as rumour, absenteeism and decreased work rates.

Emotional management means understanding that in difficult situations employees manage their emotions by seeking affirmation from others in order to stabilize their sense of the event that has caused an emotional rupture. Employees will seek to understand the rupturing event by communicating with others, who will reflect back to them a sense of the event and the impact it has on the employee. They may discuss it at home with a supportive partner or friend. They may gossip with co-workers to see what common narrative is emerging. They may call a meeting to discuss the problem. All of these actions are coping measures, as well as ways of moving forward and dealing with the event that has occurred. This can be done in a vacuum away from leadership, or the leadership can choose to engage these emotions. I highly recommend the latter approach, hence this second zone of emotion in the Dialogue Box.

Emotional management

Emotional management is a dimension of internal communications that is overlooked, but it ought to be part of the core competency of managers as communicators. Managing people is about managing emotions as well, and communications can go a long way to dealing with emotional concerns, and preventing problems from festering or escalating. Emotions are not necessarily something you see in a structured setting, such as a departmental meeting, boot camp, annual managers meeting, etc. They are more likely to surface inside meetings between colleagues, e-mail exchanges, water cooler chat and in the local watering hole. If they erupt in formal structures then you've most likely left it far too late.

To address problems in the workplace may require exploring concerns deeply bedded down in emotion, which can be approached through one-on-one meetings and peer discussions, where the concerns may surface in a more neutral way. These can then be best explored in consultative sessions rather than challenged head on. Consultative sessions are a way you can use emotional intelligence to recognize the meanings of emotions and their relationships within the workplace. Such consultation may mean dealing with a range of events going back some time into the employee's history, and it is important to see the connection of emotion to memories, since they form the bed of our emotion when we pent up our emotions, creating a whole set of source material that gets thrown into the emotional mix when the emotions erupt. In other words, we keep things bottled up.

One effect of emotion is that it can quickly lead to conversations being confrontational and ill-focused, because often the cause of the problem is unclear or difficult to locate. Taking emotion seriously in the workplace can allow you to problem-solve and resolve dissonance. Dissonance at work occurs when employees are torn between their own goals and those of the organization, or between their needs and the needs of those around them. This can lead them to get caught in a feeling of dissonance, an uncertainty about their role, skills or suitability. This is all part of the uncertainty of emotion, and the fact that employees may reflect a range of moods in the workplace. They may show anxiety or joy, energy and listlessness, participation and withdrawal. They may be in a good place emotionally when change happens, and have a can-do attitude to make the change successful. Alternatively, they can be approached with a challenge or problem and come back with defensive responses, feeling threatened or disenfranchised by the change. They may experience a state of dissonance, uncertain in their decisions or actions. They may feel under pressure, destabilized or even hurt by events around them.

In times of emotional disturbance, employees may communicate their emotions in a range of ways, such as appearing to be distracted or disconnected, or they may show anger or upset. This will depend on the individual's personality, their position and their context. I recall a staff member of a new team I had to manage who was very silent and disconnected when I discussed with the team the strategy I had planned for the department. The others seemed motivated or at least positive about the new challenges. This team member was clearly at odds, for reasons I could not know at first glance. I asked her to see me after the presentation, and we had a discussion, starting with my noting she seemed disconnected from the meeting and asking what was wrong and whether we could fix it. The outcome of the meeting was that the department had previously been mismanaged and many people had left or were forced to leave, and she figured it was only a matter of time before she had to leave. In fact, she had a great deal that was able to be harnessed and she was soon leading projects and moving far beyond what she ever imagined she could do.

The point is that emotions can communicate a lot of information, and a good emotional manager needs to be aware and keep an open mind. If someone in a meeting appears to be disconnected or distracted, their emotional state may be communicating that they don't feel they are included in what is being discussed or planned, or they may have problems at home that are impacting their work. If you observe these signs you can take a shortcut to helping them solve their problem, if you are in a position to do something about it.

Like many things in life, in the emotional world of the employee the old is framing the new. Past experiences in the workplace and how challenging situations have been resolved in the past will frame how they will respond to new challenges. If there is a commitment to change this dynamic the results will not become apparent immediately, and the employee will need ongoing support to reassure them that change is happening, and their views will need to be solicited frequently to assess that things are on the right track. This may seem high maintenance, and in some cases this may well be the case; it all depends on the individuals and the severity of the emotional disconnect being healed. No one is saying emotional management is easy! There are, however, some approaches that can help systematize the process to make the task somewhat easier, on both sides.

In a time of emotional disturbance, the emotional sense is framing the rational sense. When this happens, we need to appeal to the emotional rather than the rational. We need to communicate feelings rather than reasons. While rational communication persuades the reasoning individual, emotional communication engages the whole person. We can communicate on an emotional level when we show understanding and empathy, and see things from the other person's point of view. By showing empathy, we open the door to wisdom. To be wise in a situation means to listen. It means that we connect and value the qualities of the other person.

The outcome of this is that we cultivate sensitivity to people's situations, and they to ours. Such communication drives us to communicate the human spirit with the action, by humanizing our decisions rather than dehumanizing or depersonalizing. Even tough decisions can be made in a sensitive way, because ultimately people do understand, even if their initial reaction is emotionally negative. The issue for the emotional manager is whether they have the courage to present in person the difficult decision, and whether they have the 'thick skin' to take the blowback. Managing emotionally means allowing others to share their, and your, personal space without fear of exposure or ridicule. The problem of power, which we have discussed, is that sharing the personal space can be a means for manipulation, which means there is a journey of trust to be taken if this personal space is to be opened and remain open, rather than being a site of power.

Three steps to effective emotional management

The three steps to emotional management are:

1 acknowledgement;

2 self-identification; and

3 acceptance.

The first step – *acknowledgement* – involves each person acknowledging the legitimacy of a decision or situation, even if they disagree in whole or in part. Legitimacy here means accepting that the decision has been taken in the best interests of the organization, while accepting there may be flaws or concerns to address. Naturally these could be flagged during the formation process, but if not there should be openness at later stages to comment or criticism.

The second step – *self-identification* – means the employee seeks an understanding of where they stand within the process and identifies how the decision affects them, or whether they can identify themselves with the decision or project.

The last step is *acceptance* – either accepting their role or rejecting their role and seeking a new role elsewhere within the organization or externally. These are not necessarily easy steps, and it is not going to be a smooth journey, but this three-step approach can be used to frame discussions and communication with employees to achieve a manageable outcome.

Emotions also require us to understand our own feelings about a situation. There are few less pleasant experiences than telling someone they will no longer have a job, especially when you know there is a threat or inevitability that you will be following them out of the door. There are some managers, unfortunately, who take the cowardly position of getting one of their managers to tell someone they are being 'let go' and then only have the one conversation left, which is to tell that manager they are also to be 'let go'. This approach is a contradiction of the values organizations usually espouse, and yet it still happens. These stress situations put a strain on an organization's values, sometimes in a legitimate test that the organization passes, while at other times they expose the superficiality of the values statements boasted by the organization.

What happens when we negate empathy is simple. It can block the way by denying the value of another person or by preaching and moralizing, putting the other person in 'their place'. This is still a process of asserting power over another, which can be achieved in a number of ways. It can be done by rationalizing and being intelligent, but in a way that creates distance, avoids engagement and ignores the value of a person. It can also be done more aggressively by bullying and belittling the person. In short, non-empathetic communication tends to asserts one's self over the other. This brings it into relationship with power, both positively and negatively, because inevitably to empathize with someone means to change the role of power. In our roles, or existing relationships, there is an understanding of power. I am your boss or supervisor, or you are my superior. One has power over another, by position, negation, habit or agreement. The question is how far we are prepared to go in empathizing to change the balance of power. If I give you more time or space, open up to you, will you gain a power hold over me? For instance, to make an apology is a relational power that shifts power in the relationship. The apology can make you look weak, or it can repair damage done to the relationship.

Strategies for emotional management

Emotional management, as already mentioned, is not easy. In dealing with emotions we use a number of coping mechanisms. We can hide behind a mask in the form of a position we have in an organization, a function we perform or a role we have in a relationship. We can create distance to protect ourselves, communicating this by body language, verbal and physical positioning or verbal comments. Hence, folding our arms creates a barrier, referring to oneself as the boss or telling an employee where and when to sit is a positioning play, and criticisms of performance in certain terms can close doors to engagement very securely. Another defence mechanism is to deflect attention from ourselves by words and actions. We do this in an attempt to insulate our inner self from others or the situation. We do this to manage external and internal pressures. Coping with pressure has a lot to do with time constraints and deadlines, which can pile on pressure, particularly when they collide with pressures elsewhere. A business project can interfere with a vacation or ruin weekend plans. These are defences we need to be aware of within ourselves as emotional managers, so that we may overcome them and use more connecting and communicative strategies.

One of the most challenging emotional connections is the one between work and home. Working through emotions involves

Communicating empathy is done by using the right words, such as:

❖ I understand your needs.

❖ I can see why you are upset/offended.

❖ I know what it feels like.

❖ I'm sorry.

❖ Can we work this out?

We can communicate in a non-empathetic way by saying:

❖ I'm sorry, but you've got this all wrong.

❖ See me later.

❖ This is my project.

❖ You are wrong.

❖ You're making this a bigger deal than it is.

coping with pressures at work and at home; the famous 'work/life balance'. For managers this means they are working at a rate that affects their home life, but it can appear among other employee groups. A problem at work can be brought home and affect the home life of anyone, and vice versa. We've discussed already the affirmative role family life can play in the life of an employee, but many employees will have a difficult home life: some may be young and still living at home; others may have a situation of conflict or other demands at home, such as the need to take care of an elderly parent or a disabled child. It is not your role to get involved in these situations or become a social worker, but being sensitively aware of these demands can help your understanding of the employee and their performance at work. The hardest and most dedicated of workers can fail to perform on occasions when these demands have an event occurring that impacts their energy, spirit or time-keeping. Knowing the background can remind us to be more tolerant than we might otherwise be when the employee turns up later or is not as productive as usual.

These pressures will vary according to the rewards and needs of an individual, as well as their personal history. The pressures of work can reap great rewards for some people, and their home life is perhaps structured in a way to accept any of the inconveniences caused. Equally, a relationship may 'boil over' under pressure and cause arguments at home or performance issues at work. Coping with work creates demands on relationships, both at home and in the workplace. A supportive relationship will ease pressure and help to release any frustrations. Interrupted vacations may be seen as just part of the job, because there is reward on the horizon that makes it worthwhile, such as a promotion or a bonus. Some people thrive on the pressure, and don't mind a ruined weekend as it fills more important needs, such as recognition of one's value to the organization. On the other hand, an individual's personal history may have problems or emotional triggers that emerge under pressure. These deeper concerns may erupt under stress, and lead to poor performance or errors. The workplace is still usually seen as a place where you succeed; you do your job to the best of your abilities. It is not readily a place for failure, yet coping also means learning to live with mistakes. A lot can be learned from a manager's style, and the values of individuals and organizations, in how they deal with mistakes. Some will punish, others will tolerate; some may see learning opportunities, while others may offer support mechanisms.

Emotions are at the heart of many difficult personal issues, including depression, worrying about the kids, the aforementioned relationship issues, and status envy. The last of these merits a little discussion here. Our work is an important part of our status; it says something about who we are: white collar or blue collar, senior director or middle manager, leader or led, public official or householder, etc. The wealth we gain from our work makes a difference to the house we own, the car we drive, the places we vacation and the schools our kids go to, etc. These are all aspects of social status, and can be the cause of status envy or anxiety. These are very personal to the individual, because we all have different wants and interests, but they are a big part of what makes people tick. Positively, these interests or desires can spur ambition, while negatively, they can put pressure on people when they find what they want to be beyond their grasp. There is no magic bullet for this issue, so it is important to be aware of this discussion as part of the emotional mix. These desires and appetites are part of motivation.

Motivational emotions

I have perhaps placed a little more focus on the negative side of emotion for most of this chapter, and for good reason. It is an aspect of communication most ignored or least understood, and for this reason I venture there are more emotional problems of a negative nature in organizations than there are positive ones. There are, of course, many motivational books, videos and speakers that will tell you how to motivate your staff, and much of it probably works. However, most of these are aimed at individuals who are leaders, telling them how to motivate themselves and their teams in one big, happy session. I want to contest this, and suggest that we need a deeper and more nuanced approach to emotions, and to recognize across the whole organization the difficulty and sensitivity of this area of human life. We need to know the dark side of our employee emotions if we are to understand the fully human nature of communication and engagement. These individuals we call employees come to work every day, bringing their hopes, dreams, problems and last night's fight with them. They do not simply leave these things at the door when they clock on or off at the workplace. They are concerns and desires that they carry with them through the day, achieving highs and lows in the workplace. In other words, these emotions are in dialogue with the workplace emotions.

Difficult organizational issues are tied to the emotions in the workplace. The anxiety and sense of well-being comes clearly into focus when we look at aspects of organizational life such as performance measurement, cut-backs, people leaving the organization, recruitment, business successes and failures, and new management. All of these raise questions in employees about their role and value in the organization. In performance management terms we want to do well, and may disagree with the evaluation we are given. When cut-backs occur we wonder if will lose our job. When people leave we wonder if we are stuck in a rut while others move on to bigger or better things. When the business is successful and expanding then employees will feel some of the good, while they will feel concern and perhaps depression when the business slumps in a recession. When new management comes in we wonder how our role will be affected or whether we will succeed under the new style of management. All these release emotion within the organization, person by person.

This is the complex emotional organization you are in dialogue with, which is multifaceted and ever-changing. This means that you need to be sensitive to the nuances of individual and group behaviour. You have to learn to profile your organization as an emotional one, and match this against the messages that you are communicating. The problem with purely intelligent communications is that it behaves as if the organization is normatively logical and calm, receptive to the message, with many management assumptions being taken as normative for the workforce at large. The suggestion in this chapter is that this is not the case, and often your employees are emotionally disengaged or remote from the hopes, dreams and enthusiasms of the C-Suite. The emotional state of the organization forms the bed of the variety of interpretations that employees will draw from significant events within the organization, which takes us into the next zone in our Dialogue Box – interpretation.

Questions

1   Can you recall examples of employee emotions running high? What were the chief causes? How was this handled by the leadership? Did the communication engage with the emotional issues effectively? How could the emotional issues have been avoided, and how could they have been engaged with more effectively?

2   Is it possible for you to define the current emotional state of your organization? Are there differences across the organization? Can you look at the leaders in various areas and see how their management style helps or hinders emotional management?

3   How much human capital do you believe your leadership has to spend? Let's do a little scenario-playing. If a major crisis or event impacts employees emotionally, do you believe there is sufficient trust and connection for employees to be convinced by the party line offered by

leadership? Imagine two or three types of events, and try to gauge your answers.

4   Think of the three steps to effective emotional management, namely acknowledgement, self-identification and acceptance; do you see this pattern being effective? Look at your examples of emotional events in question 1; can you use these steps to answer the first question more fully?

5   Look at how you use words; do you always appreciate the emotional baggage that particular words carry? Think of some emotional situations you've been in, and write down the words and phrases you remember. How much were you seeking to make the event more or less emotional, and how would you change your language upon reflection?

07

Zone 3: Interpretation – how organizations and people understand

C ompanies, like individuals, believe they are being clear when they communicate, but this is not always the case. There are many elements, including context, experience, knowledge and mood, which can determine how someone interprets the information they receive. The individual is both a spectator and an agent. As Adam Smith, author of *The Wealth of Nations,* explained it:

> When I endeavour to examine my own conduct... I divide myself, as it were, into two persons; and that I, the examiner and judge, represent a different character from the other I, the person whose conduct is examined into and judged of. The first is **the spectator**... The second is **the agent,** the person whom I properly call myself, and of whose conduct, under the character of a spectator, I was endeavoring to form some opinion.

Interpretation is pivotal in the Dialogue Box (see Figure 7.1), as it derives from the intelligence and emotions of the individual being

FIGURE 7.1 The Dialogue Box: Focus on Interpretation

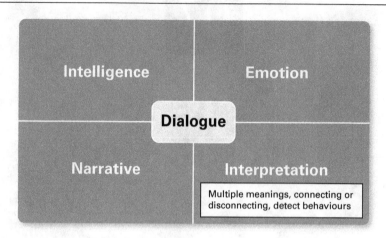

synthesized into an understanding, an interpretation, of events within the organization. All the intelligence an individual receives can be contradicted when mediated by the emotional reception of this intelligence, seen from the viewpoint of individuals, even to the point of facts being contradicted or trumped by feelings and spin. Sometimes the employee will be a spectator, but when it comes to events affecting them they become the complex agents Adam Smith was writing about. Like emotion, this is a subjective decision, and so is as multifaceted and ever-changing as the emotional states we discussed in the last chapter. It is also pivotal in the Dialogue Box because in the act of interpretation, we seek to control meaning.

What is interpretation?

We can see two different major categories of interpretation; the talk about something and explaining the meaning of that thing. They are connected with one another, but in talking about something we are essentially signifying that it means something without defining it. To say what something means, on the other hand, we are offering an interpretation; we are filling the thing with meaning. Thus if I point to a dog and say, 'There is a dog', I am simply pointing out and stating something I see. However, if I talk about the dog then I will be interpreting whether it is a nice dog, a mean dog, a dog on the loose and so on. These are all descriptions that go beyond the mere statement of the dog before me, and may be contested, for we may have different ideas or knowledge about the dog. If we apply this to employees, I may state, 'There is a lathe worker', or, 'there's Joan from accounts', and this is simply a description of the function of the person's job. However, I may say, 'There is a lathe worker; we have safety issues in his shop', or, 'There's Joan from accounts; she always looks so furtive', and this is a start to offering or inviting invitations to interpretation.

We interpret subjectively and objectively. The subjective involves reading what we understand, or want to understand, into a situation. We interpret from our own viewpoint, assumptions and prejudices. The objective means we are trying to understand the truth of the matter, giving a fair viewpoint to all agents in the situation, of which we may count as one. In the workplace we have vested interests in decisions, changes and strategies; it is, after all, our livelihood. We may be pleased when the president and CEO announce new record profits, because we might see a pay rise or a bonus, perhaps new investment in our workplace and some air-conditioning! In the subjective sense of interpretation we are interpreting as agent, but we also have the capacity to interpret objectively, as spectator. This is important, because it is at this juncture that we can connect intelligently with the individual employee. When there is a major recession and employees are being laid off, then the intelligent employee will understand the necessity of this and be prepared to some extent for their own possible exit, though they may not be happy about this. It is at this point that we can approach employees and have a constructive dialogue, but this assumes we have not set them emotionally apart in the first place.

In the example of a recessionary set of redundancies, we can see the possibility of constructive dialogue but this will not happen, or at best will be severely set back, if we have not gone about it in the right way. Announcing a redundancy plan to the media before employees is one way to create distance. Another way is to give inadequate preparation to the employee announcement and not providing training to managers to make the announcement in a sensitive and responsive way. The Dialogue Box will help you to do this, as we will explore later. What can happen is that employees' emotional responses to the announcement create a barrier to understanding the leadership, and give more credence to negative interpretations of events. Let's try another example. The company has announced a major reorganization and people are being moved or dismissed as a result. Let's assume this was announced in the wrong manner, perhaps via the media first. Employees are in an uproar and deeply unsettled, wondering what's going to happen to them. The company is in a state of instability. Various interpretations of everyday events will emerge. One day, an employee – let's call him Fred – sees another employee, Deborah, in a meeting with a senior manager, courtesy of a fishbowl office. The exchanges are animated, and Deborah looks much more lively than is her normal demeanour. This event is open to many interpretations. Given Fred's emotional state, and the instability of the company, Fred may well interpret that the meeting is about Deborah getting fired, and so he tells other employees what he thinks is happening. At the same time, Maria sees them together and has heard rumours of an affair, because the manager and Deborah work so closely together. Maria may be less concerned about the layoffs – perhaps her job is safe – and so she thinks they are breaking it off, or having a lovers' tiff. This interpretation may have nothing to do with the emotional state of the company, but may provide light relief to Fred's tragic tale. Yet, Fred and Maria are seeing the same thing; it's just they are working from different assumptions and paying attention to different aspects of life, grounded in their different emotional states.

Now, let's move the story on. Let's say the truth of the situation is that the manager and Deborah are having a discussion about a new project that will boost her department and she is being asked to take on major new responsibilities. Her animated response is a mixture of excitement for the challenge but also concern about how her team will be able to meet the challenge with some of the layoffs affecting her department. She may not be ready to announce this to her team, and has to continue strategic planning until everything is approved and signed off. In the meantime, rumours of an affair and the apparent inevitability of her departure are circulating in the company as viable interpretations, affecting people's view of her, the department and the company as a whole. Same event, different interpretations in circulation – we'll come back to this later.

The reason different interpretations emerged in our illustrative scenarios is due to the subjective nature of observation and interpretation.

This is not, however, the key issue. What makes these interpretations challenging is the authority assigned to the interpretations. The starting point is the individual making the claims. If Fred is seen as unreliable and prone to exaggerating things or being a gossip then his interpretation may not fly far, whatever the emotional state of the organization. If Maria is known to have been Deborah's friend and they had a falling-out a while back or is known to have conspiracy theories for everything, then we have the same outcome as in Fred's case. A further level of challenge is that the healthier the organization the less likely there will be various authoritative interpretations. The question is thus, what interpretation trumps the others?

When we interpret we look for both verbal and non-verbal signs. The meaning of the words we speak are mediated by tone of voice and physical actions, so even though we may choose our words carefully they will be mediated by tone and body language to determine the ultimate meaning, which either supports what we intended or results in our words being modified. An obvious example is that we say we are excited for someone but then our tone of voice and body language actually suggest we are not in the least bit interested, or are jealous, or some other underlying sense of what we are truly thinking. Of course, we can become good actors able to disguise our true self, but even then the slightest nuance out of step might give the game away. We can also communicate without words. If I look at my watch during a meeting there may be any number of things I am communicating, and the interpretation will be affected by many things. I may be bored, late for another meeting, impatient, idly curious, keeping track of how the meeting is progressing, all manner of options just with one gesture. We need more than the gesture to fill out the picture, and we look for other signs and subsequent behaviour to judge why the gesture was made; even then the answer may never be clear. We may rely on other information we have about the person and the context of the meeting, in order to interpret the gesture, which may be a simple but telling one.

In the process of interpreting we are also seeking to divine the truth of statements and signs, and as we make up our mind about how we are interpreting an event there is a process by which the credibility of statements and information gains a stronghold and starts to guide our deliberations. This is important when people are trying to influence us, because they can make an early strike at a person or a source of information by promoting their cause or undermining their credibility. In this way, divining the truth of statements and signs is steered in a particular direction, and it can be hampered as we can stumble towards the truth or fall into error. In addition, how we interpret events in part depends upon our prior understanding and the assumptions we make. If we think someone is bad at their job and they make a mistake, we will interpret the mistake differently, certainly less generously, than we would with someone we admire. Those who seek to influence us will try to detect these underlying assumptions, and either build on them or seek to destabilize them in order to influence our opinions and decisions. However, it is also possible that by holding a particular bias or being prejudiced our prior understanding and assumptions will remain unchallenged by new information or events.

When we face a difficult or demanding situation, what we see is complexity, wherein exists nuance. We live, in this sound-bite age, in a world that seems to allow very little room for nuance. We also live in a fast-changing world where there just doesn't seem time for complexity. Faced as we are with complexity and contradictions, we naturally try to discern patterns in behaviour and seek to make rapid sense of events and information we receive. We try to simplify and make information easily digestible, so people will respond quickly and act in the way we want them to act. However, we should embrace complexity, while at the same time eschewing making things complicated. This is not to say we should dumb things down; the philosopher Ludwig Wittgenstein said: 'Any intelligent fool can make things bigger, more complex, and more violent. It takes a touch of genius – and a lot of courage – to move in the opposite direction.' This is what I mean here by embracing complexity. Other advocates for this approach to complexity include E F Schumacher, who said: 'The aspects of things that are most important to us are hidden because of their simplicity and familiarity', and Albert Einstein, who said: 'Everything should be made as simple as possible, but not simpler.'

The key of meaning

The Scottish psychiatrist R D Laing related an incident in his work, explaining how the hospital he was at in Glasgow had a female patient who sat rocking back and forth in her chair, naked and mumbling incoherently. None of the doctors knew how to reach her. Laing observed the woman for some time before taking off his own clothes, sitting down opposite her and rocking in harmony with her and making similar verbal sounds. The woman started to communicate for the first time since entering the hospital, leaving Laing to ask his colleagues if it ever occurred to them to start from where she was situated, from where she was suffering. Not that I would recommend this in your organization; the point of the story is that Laing was seeking to understand what level of meaning he had to reach in order to connect with the woman. On another level, we instinctively do this with children when we crouch down to talk to them at their level, to make eye contact and not to appear as a 'big person'. Organizationally, we sometimes have to figure out the level we need to communicate at in order to connect in a meaningful way. Hierarchy may help organize but it also creates barriers to meaning, sets us apart, and there are occasions when we need to understand this and break out of the hierarchy or normal order of organizational life.

Many years ago I recall watching an exceptionally awful movie, which happily my memory has all but erased save for one thing: the characters, when faced with difficulty or confusion, kept saying, 'Give it a name.' This saying stayed with me, because naming is important to how we frame meaning and the key to interpretation is meaning; in other words we are looking at signs and attempting to determine their meaning and 'give it a name'. On one level, the meaning of a statement may be clear, and often we take things at their face value for convenience or because that is all there is to it. Naming in organizations, in the media and in popular debate can be used as a shorthand way of determining that something will be understood in a particular way. Jargon is used for this purpose, and so is corporate language peculiar to a particular organization. Politicians and political campaigns understand this when they seek to control the agenda with meaning and language.

While naming things, by which I also mean jargon and catchphrases, can be good shorthand for describing functions, activities, etc, it can also lead to inhibiting creativity. If we take the example of 'corporate social responsibility', we can see how there has been a battle over meaning. Initially it became a term covering 'Good PR', as companies sought to appear as good corporate citizens. They hired people from non-governmental organizations to add some credibility, but found there was a lot of political baggage that came with these new professionals, who demanded companies take CSR issues more seriously. What started out as an exercise in ticking the box became a serious internal debate. Some companies change CSR to just CR, while others debate what we mean by 'sustainability', arguing that being sustainable as a business means ensuring the company will be here in 10, 20 years and beyond. Just as meaning can be used to tick boxes, it can also be used to block work. Work is blocked by naming it and thinking we have done it, so no added budget or effort is put into it, just enough to suggest the organization has it under control. The other effect this can have is that it can lead to discounting. By having a word or term assign the meaning of something it gets corralled into irrelevance, as people discount its effect or importance, again a facet of the 'ticking the box' mentality. Such 'discounting' plagues internal communications, which to an extent is the ultimate discounted function in the organization.

The problem is that naming can lead to lazy thinking or diminished understanding of a complex event, person or situation. In our communications age, an era where we are deluged by communication, we continually face complexity, and as a result there is a drive to name things so that we can readily understand them, because we are too overloaded or lazy to do otherwise. While naming is also a means to box and control meaning, occasionally the genie escapes from the bottle and meaning eludes us. We need to take a deeper dive than this into meaning, and I apologize beforehand for using some thinkers from other fields to explain myself, but meaning is itself a meaningful study and benefits from being painted on a broad canvas. Once we dive deeper into meaning then we can see that when we interpret we are seeking to determine whether someone's actions or words are revealing or concealing. It is often said that memos are written to defend the sender rather than inform the receiver, and there is some truth in this, because when we communicate we sometimes seek to reveal something or hide it. Otherwise, why communicate?

We have already discussed how, in trying to make sense, we try to systematize situations, and will often fill in the gaps in our data, which can be effective but also disastrous. Being able to fill in gaps can help us to understand a situation or project a strategy in a situation, which is essential in dealing with elements we might not know for sure. We make assumptions to fill in the gaps and try to define what seems to be a natural trajectory, thereby creating what can be a self-fulfilling trajectory for our thoughts. Meaning plays a role in this, because words and terms can be used to fill in the gaps. Such meanings can work across the organization to describe an individual or unit, and hence a successful interpretation or popularly accepted meaning becomes currency in the marketplace of organizational morale, as negative or positive interpretations can lead to an undermining or uplifting of spirits in the organization.

As a result, this zone of interpretation is the litmus test for detecting behavioural breakdown within the organization. If the impact of a decision or strategy results in a successful outcome, it is more likely there will be an interpretation that matches the decision or strategy circulating within the organization. However, if the impact is a negative one then there will simply be multiple negative interpretations or meanings increasingly in circulation that will highlight the fact that you have a problem. There are more negative interpretations in circulation than positive, because human nature lends itself to telling negative stories more than positive – just look at news reporting for testimony to this conclusion. If we take the example of the reorganization announcement, we know there is an emotional reaction that will yield interpretations. At this point, the signs of a problem are there to be seen early on and the task of internal communications is to learn to detect breakdown at this stage, not wait for zone 4, when a core counter-narrative has taken hold.

However, this is not just a negative zone, though much focus is on the negative because, as noted, varied interpretations emerge during difficult times. There is the possibility of achieving a more positive emotional engagement with employees, based on the notion that one of our human qualities is our aspirational desire. We want to achieve more, get more, and experience more. We look to the horizon of our desires, but the world between us and this horizon is complex and the terrain challenging. The role of values within an organization is critical here. If the values are only a 'PR gimmick' then they will remain only words. We have to fill them with meaning at a deep level, and provide support to managers to embrace their meaning and implement them within their sphere of management. You need to be asking your managers what their value horizon is, and demonstrating that how they behave takes you towards or away from your organization's value horizon. This is not a big blue sky thing; this is a case of making a renewal of commitment to manage consistent with the values on a daily basis. We each start the day deciding what we want or have to do that day, but at the end of the day do we reflect effectively on what we have done in relation to our values horizon?

As with the other zones, internal communications here does not simply mean the department or function; it means leadership, managers, supervisors and all employees throughout the organization. This requires managers to get involved to help employees struggling with the issues, helping to reframe these issues, and having their ear to the ground. The easiest route to reaching resolution of difficulties is in the early stages before the emotions become hardened into entrenched positions. There is more room for negotiation at this point through open communication and dialogue. This work on values has to start with the C-Suite. I've said it before, and it is worth repeating: good and bad behaviours emanate from the C-Suite. This is because the C-Suite authorizes good and bad behaviours by behaving as such themselves, or allowing them to go unnoticed in the organization. Likewise, the C-Suite rewards good and bad behaviours by recognizing them or promoting them. If a leader behaves in one way then they must expect those they manage to take their lead on behaviour from them. Actions become acceptable or not acceptable accordingly. The power to change behaviour thus lies with the C-Suite setting an example, letting good behaviours emanate from the C-Suite, while being clear on stamping out bad behaviours. These good behaviours will be imitated in a ripple effect across the organization. In these ways behaviours are given meaning, and their meaning can be heard throughout the organization. To be rude to one of your direct reports means they can be rude to their reports or colleagues.

Meaning to connect

Meaning and interpretation are about connections we make. When people get in the work lift in the morning and talk about last night's television they are connecting through something in common that has meaning, albeit trivial. If we did not see last night's television we do not join in so readily, we do not connect. Talking about the weather, a sport, all of these things are ritual openings to connection, starting with meaningful things at a base and largely neutral level. People are connecting before they get on with the meaningful stuff of work. They are outside of the boundaries of work for a short while before they become 'positions', 'bosses', 'functions' or 'department members'. I like the description of meaning offered by the French philosopher Michel Foucault, who used the image of the sea washing onto the shore to describe the transgressive nature of language and the complexity of defining boundaries. The sea can wash away or wash up debris, leaves a different shoreline with each lap on the sand, and can wipe away words written in the sand. Language does this. Language does more than simply describe or communicate; it affects the way we look at the world and the way we respond to other people. This means our boundaries are not so clear either. The organization defines boundaries for work, but relationships and connections between people will mean that these boundaries are not necessarily fixed. There will be closer connections between some people, and some people seem to 'get away with murder' when it comes to the boss, have more influence within the team, are more or less popular, have an undeserved bad reputation and so on.

I will leave you with a puzzling reflection on meaning. *The Trial*, by Kafka, is the story of a guard, called the door-keeper, and a man who waits a number of years for entry through the door of the law. Arguably, Kafka is one of the writers par excellence on interpretation and meaning, but I will just offer a tiny portion of his work. The story is really a parable told by a priest to K, who has been arrested for reasons he never quite grasps. The parable tells how the man is seeking entry through what is called the door of the law, but is denied. For many years he seeks entry, all the time asking questions about the door and what lies behind it. The parable concludes:

> Before he dies, all that he has experienced during the whole time of his sojourn condenses in his mind into one question, which he has never yet put to the door-keeper. He beckons the door-keeper, since he can no longer raise his stiffening body. The door-keeper has to bend far down to hear him, for the difference in size between them has increased very much to the man's disadvantage. 'What do

you want to know now?' asks the door-keeper, 'you are insatiable.' 'Everyone strives to attain the Law', answers the man, 'how does it come about, then, that in all these years no one has come seeking admittance but me?' The door-keeper perceives that the man is nearing his end and his hearing is failing, so he bellows in his ear: 'No one but you could gain admittance through this door, since this door was intended only for you. I am now going to shut it.'

Kafka probably doesn't feature too often in communication and management books, but because we are talking about meaning it is, I suggest, helpful for us to take a little philosophical and literary detour. I have offered some thought-provoking ideas, but you will no doubt have some of your own that you've read in the past. You can go back to these thinkers and see how their ideas relate to the way you think about meaning, because as much as we think we are clear, the truth is that often we are not. The issues of meaning and interpretation are among the most complex elements in human life and in the life of the organization. Meaning is subject to emotional, psychological, political, spiritual and philosophical norms, and what we find meaningful is not the same as our neighbour or work colleague. We may want to keep things rational or managerial in our understanding of the organization, but these various thinkers, ideas and Kafka's parable are a reminder that in internal communications we are also dealing with individuals and what is meaningful in their lives. Kafka, like all great novelists, was a master narrator, and it is to narrative that we now turn.

Questions

1   Think of some recent events that have been controversial or misunderstood in your organization, and assess the various interpretations that people offered as to what was the problem. How do these fit with the leadership narrative and with your own version of events?

2   How often do you find different interpretations surrounding events in your organization? Are there many instances, or just a few?

3   Does your organization, and communications, use lots of jargon? In meetings are there many occasions where language and stories are used

to include or exclude people? Pay attention in your next few meetings to how language and jargon are used.

4   Turning to the more philosophical question of meaning, how can you make communication more meaningful in your organization? In areas such as values, ethics and sustainability, do you think the right words are being used, or is it merely that the words are being used uncritically?

5   How often do you look to other sources, such as literary, philosophical and spiritual ideas, to give insight to the meaning of your work and the organization? Is there much conflict, or are they closely related? When you interpret events in the organization, to what extent do you think you are drawing on these other sources, rather than the messages of leadership or organizational lore?

08

Zone 4: Narrative – how organizations and people agree (or disagree!)

Within your organization there is a whole lot of communicating going on. People are constantly communicating, and this communication is as much a part of 'corporate communications' as the communications department. In the process of this communication there are a variety of stories being told, to entertain or inform. There are stories that reinforce good things going on in the organization, and stories that lower the morale of employees. Just as in life generally, at any given time there are people who are happy in an organization and people who are not so happy, perhaps worse. We are all storytellers. We tell our story, which becomes part of other people's stories, which then get passed on. All we can ever do is tell our story, but by passing this on it becomes part of a continuing narrative that is greater than us as individuals. These stories form an overarching narrative that describes what is going on in the organization or in the life of employees. Essentially, narrative is an agreed story of the organization, which may disagree with the leadership's intended narrative and even the truth, but it is the agreed version of events according to the majority of employees. We can go beyond a specific decision or strategy and study the context of an organization to discover that the narrative of the organization may be systemic, revealing something about the organization such as a high level of morale and positive energy or a deep crisis of morale and an organizational neurosis.

When we looked at the intelligence zone, we saw that the outcome of all the work that companies and leadership do to create a strategy or effect a decision generates a certain narrative. The leadership seeks to establish a core narrative, which tells of a successful strategy, a spirit of excellence, and so on. When we got into zone 2, we saw that the emotional response can derail this narrative and give rise in zone 3 to various interpretations about what is 'really going on'. In zone 4, if the leadership narrative has not taken root then we will detect another narrative, what is called a counter-narrative, which emerges from the emotional response and the various interpretations circulating within the organization. The various interpretations, feeding off the emotional state, become supportive or contrary to narrative strands, including the official narrative. As these interpretations get absorbed and added to other details or information then various narratives emerge or will lose traction in tandem, resulting in one narrative emerging to become the core counter-narrative. In the context of multiple narratives emerging, we need to appreciate that these narratives compete. In planning and running any organization, the leadership, in communicating with employees, aims to foster a certain narrative, but this narrative can be overturned by stronger narrative claims on employees, and these contradictory narratives can damage morale, or simply act as a brake on aspirations. Positively speaking, contradictory narratives can critique and strengthen the company narrative.

We can ask whether narrative is clear like glass or more like a diamond. We can use narrative in both ways. We can use it to make the truth of a situation clear like glass. We can also use narrative like a diamond, using elements to highlight particular aspects, to dazzle, and perhaps to distract. A truthful narrative is clear like glass, not a diamond, and it should show the truth as clearly as possible and not be turned in the light to highlight different perceptions of the truth. The truth should captivate, keeping the attention of your employees. A narrative of truth and integrity gives less room for counter-narrative, and should be able to trump challenging narratives as much as possible. If you only offer positive and motivational stories to employees then you devalue the narrative elements of your over-arching story. The character and storylines become less credible in this case, as people expect to see ups and downs in the story, and expect some inherent contradictions or challenges to the main narratives. It is this process of understanding that gives credence to many narratives. In other words, if it sounds too good to be true then it is probably false. Employees respond to narratives that engage them and will participate in the ongoing story, while narrative that 'talks at' them creates only silence and disengagement.

What is narrative?

Narrative is much more than simply telling stories (see Figure 8.1). When narrative and storytelling are first presented to managers, as in my introductory comments, there can often be a response of scepticism. Like communications generally, it is not seen as a hard science or as being about concrete aspects of the organization. Communications remains, in the eyes of some managers, still as a case of 'telling others what we do' or 'spinning' a story. Yet think back to the examples in the Introduction – what narrative triumphed? The HMV narrative was about the firings, the BP story about the oil spill. The narrative battle was not won by the leadership; instead they were placed in a position of responding to a narrative dictated by others. In the HMV case it was the fired employees, and in the BP case it was the media. Imagine a major event or crisis occurring within your organization. How would you plan for it? If you have been through a crisis, look back and assess the narrative that developed. Any surprises? We will come back to these examples in the concluding chapter. Happily, after time is spent on the Dialogue Box there is a realization among managers who have run through scenarios that understanding stories in the organization is a much more significant matter than might appear at first glance. We need to understand narrative on two levels. At one level, narratives are stories that individuals tell that can illuminate, contradict, challenge, inform and so on. Your organization has a great number of narratives or stories being told as you read this. They may be stories about people, about customers, the organization; the list goes on. There is the other level, and this is the bird's-eye view level of narrative. What is happening to the organization or to an individual? This is the objective or major narrative that emerges out of the stories circulating in the organization. It can be the truth or it can be a consensus about what the majority thinks is going on. We will come back to this, but first we need to explore the notion of stories.

We have all grown up with stories. Our parents and teachers read us stories. We have made up and written stories. We use stories to express our imagination. There is something about storytelling that appeals to us all; it is a part of being human. What we can grasp about narrative is that there is something intuitive about stories, because they touch nerves in our human nature and we all use narrative as storytelling to some degree, to illuminate an event or something about human nature. However, the storytelling does more than illuminate the story; it also sheds light on the storyteller. Hearing the kinds of stories people tell, and the way they tell them, can reveal much about them, their work and those they are in relationships with. Narrative informs our relationships, and causes us to change our dealings with other people, allowing us to know another person or to understand our relationship to them. We may think someone respects our work, but then we discover some new piece of knowledge that tells us they do not. Perhaps they have told us what we want to hear or they have manipulated us; in both cases we have been persuaded they have our interests in mind. The new knowledge may be an e-mail they sent to our boss that puts us in a bad light, may be an 'off the cuff' remark designed to undermine or it may be spread as a rumour. If there are malicious stories circulating about someone there is a good chance we hear these stories before we meet that person, and our approach to them is often highly influenced by these received stories. Equally, we may be told impressive stories about someone that influence how we approach them, and we may be more impressed than the person deserves or made less confident in our approach to this person. The point is that narrative is selective and interpretive. Stories are told to persuade us to think about a particular person, thing or event in a particular way. The story or narrative is not an obvious objective telling that tells us all we need to know. What we already know, and the way we look at things, will determine how we approach and understand a narrative.

How we tell stories

In both our personal and work lives we tell stories of all kinds. We tell funny stories, or talk about an office romance, conspiratorially set up a thriller and so on. Like novels and movies, the stories we tell have a definite narrative structure, and so we tell stories that have actors, character types and fit within dramatic categories. We use these characters, or attribute these characteristics, to build our narrative into a more impactful or fuller narrative. Our stories also have mood, events and other elements, but the key structure is the three elements of actor, character type and dramatic category; so, for example:

✤ Actor: the boss.

✤ Character type: the serious guy.

✤ Dramatic category: thriller.

Elements of storytelling

In the narrative we are being *actors*, individuals playing a role:

✤ the boss;

✤ colleague;

✤ friend;

✤ customer;

✤ shareholder; or

✤ journalist.

In our narrative we also have *character types*, such as:

✤ the comedian;

✤ the introvert;

✤ the extrovert;

✤ the serious guy;

✤ the flirt;

+ the depressive;

+ the cynic;

+ the villain; or

+ the good guy.

Commonly, narratives fall into *dramatic categories*:

+ thriller;

+ crime story;

+ action;

+ tragedy;

+ romance; or

+ comedy.

Taking these elements we can tell a story about how the boss, always serious, wanted to know who had leaked information to the media. We then embellish this to make it into a thriller where we talk about who it might be and what events led up to the leak, and then we offer a conclusion: the boss is paranoid, there's some secret deal being done, or wherever we want our narrative to lead. Let's try another example, with two actors this time:

+ Actors: colleague and customer.

+ Character types: the comedian and the serious guy.

+ Dramatic category: tragedy.

These elements are used to tell the story of Joe, a rival I want to undermine, who is known to like a joke now and then, so I can play off that. I tell a story about how Joe told an off-colour joke to a customer, who my audience knows is a serious person, and I can imply the joke offended them. This is a tragedy because we tell our audience how it made Joe, and the company, look bad. My audience feels a mixture of the humour and tragic aspects, which I can play off to make Joe actually look like the villain of the piece, and hence discredit him. The story may be skewed or embellished a great deal to get the effect I want. The truth may have been that Joe told the customer a joke that the customer just didn't get or find funny, because he is a serious guy. This may be uncomfortable for Joe, but how far does it represent a problem or a tragedy? Well, that's up to the storyteller. Perhaps there is someone there who comes up with a story to trump this, saying she was there and witnessed it as just a joke that fell flat. I think you get the picture, and we will build on this point later when we discuss counter-narratives.

Narrative is what captivates us by drawing us into the story. It makes the difference between good stories and bad stories; it is all in the telling. In a captivating narrative we put ourselves into the story, imagining what we would do or think or feel, or deciding how we feel about the actors and the drama that is being unfolded for us. Hence, a new narrative emerges out of situations to illuminate events that we are participants in, and we might find ourselves part of the narrative. The story may include us directly as a participant, or indirectly as a member of a department or organization, or a close friend or colleague of the narrative characters. Or the narrative may move on from this point, as the fact of me being told may help to embellish the story, and so I may add new elements to the story or I may give it credibility and authority. 'David thought it was shocking' may help to elevate the story for others who know me or my position within the organization. We can then see that narrative as storytelling is not simply someone telling a defined story; there is also narrative that unfolds to reveal things to us, a narrative that forms in our mind or is created by numerous conversations, and it can form part of a continuum. In advancing our narrative, the storyteller seeks out those who can add to their narrative, giving them more input or affirmation of the story elements, thereby boosting confidence in the narrative. This adding to the narrative also helps us systematize something we might be struggling to understand or derive some pleasure from having our point of view, our understanding of the narrative, reinforced. We see this in sayings such as 'misery loves company' or 'the way things are done around here', sayings that affirm our reading of the narrative. Such a sense of pessimism can spread as the narrative becomes more coherent and credible, even though it may not necessarily be true.

Counter-narrative

The organization, in reaching a decision or making an announcement, is seeking to establish a particular narrative, and either expects or hopes the internal audience will embrace this narrative and make it its own. However, organizational life is such that this does not often or easily happen. What can happen, especially when the internal audience is unsettled emotionally with lots of different interpretations doing the rounds, is that a counter-narrative starts to emerge. What I mean by a counter-narrative is a narrative that counters the truth or fallacy of a core narrative. The organization in its planning has defined a core narrative, and what emerges among employees and external parties may be a set of counter-narratives that challenge what the organization wants to be understood by a decision or plan.

A counter-narrative does not necessarily speak to the truth of the situation. It is merely a narrative that for whatever reason challenges the narrative set out by the leadership. The counter-narrative will be informed by employees' emotions and may reveal their distrust or animosity towards the leadership. This sense then creates a counter-narrative that either doubts the veracity of the original narrative or offers an alternative narrative, and this can be either true or false. A false counter-narrative seeks to establish a truth distinct from the original narrative and results in a triumph of interpretation over substance. Meanwhile a truthful counter-narrative seeks a triumph of substance over a particular interpretation. A counter-narrative, whether true or false, attempts to attract negative support. It is challenging the positive message being advanced by the organization. And however the leadership feels about their positive message, in objective reality a positive message can be true or false.

The emergence of counter-narratives can confuse loyalties, as employees are invited to choose sides. In a healthy debate, where different challenges are being laid down, this can be a productive exercise. The problem arises when the counter-narrative crowds out the truth on both sides. The existence of such a counter-narrative should highlight to the leadership there is a confrontational problem, yet it can all too often be simply misread as employees not understanding the original narrative or that it will be solved by constantly reiterating the leadership message. The need at this point is to see that the counter-narrative reveals a deeper disconnect, fissure or psychosis in the organization that needs to be met in a much more sophisticated way. To do this, we need to delve deeper into the elements of narrative.

We talked earlier of the three basic elements of storytelling, and it is time now to build these into the set of narrative elements that exist in the stories we tell. These are essentially:

- ✤ facts;
- ✤ characters;
- ✤ situations;
- ✤ events; and
- ✤ wisdom.

These elements are, to a large extent, things that an analysis of the narrative can agree upon on one level. Let me take an example of a company announcing a restructuring plan. Let's apply the story elements I set out earlier as the facts of the situation:

- ✤ Facts – restructuring announcement.
- ✤ Characters – CEO, employee.
- ✤ Situations – employee in meeting with CEO.
- ✤ Events – an employee is dismissed.
- ✤ Wisdom – impact on the company.

In this illustration, we can see that none of these elements can be contested. The company has made such an announcement – fact. We have selected two characters who work for the company – fact. There has been a meeting between the employee and the CEO – fact. The employee was subsequently dismissed – fact. The last element is the tricky one, because this is where we begin to understand how narrative has become interpretive. It is interpretive in the sense that in this story it could be that the dismissal has alarmed people, but why? It may cause unrest, but why? The point is that we may be able to state objectively the collective wisdom in response to the dismissal, irrespective of the truth of the narrative that uses these elements.

So in our story, we have a restructuring plan announced. We draw in our characters, the CEO and an employee, who meet and subsequently the employee is dismissed. The question that jumps out, or should jump out at us, is this: are these all related? The meeting may have been on another subject, and perhaps it was another meeting that preceded the dismissal. The employee may have been dismissed for some action that had nothing to do with the restructuring. Whatever the facts of the reason, the wisdom value within the company has become compromised and different interpretations have emerged to inform an alternative wisdom as to what is happening or what is best for the organization. This narrative builds on the various interpretations that have been circulating around the company, so that where you find set or competing versions of the story you will find that certain interpretive stories become part of the counter-narrative, which can become the dominant narrative.

The dominant narrative is not an 'official' narrative, nor will it necessarily jump out at you. It may take time for the dominant narrative to emerge from competing narratives and counter-narratives. However, even a cursory forensic search can enable you to piece together a dominant narrative from the stories people tell, and how they tell these stories. You will find there is a consistent set of stories, which seem to fit with the 'facts' and match the characters. In developing a consistency, there is a process of validating new stories that ensures they either become part of the dominant narrative, or are rejected. This means key figures will embrace the narrative, and other events will occur that appear to validate the emerging counter-narrative to effect its position of becoming the dominant, or accepted, narrative. These dominant stories thus create a new and guiding grand narrative. While the planning and thinking process we discussed in the intelligence zone assumes the role of dominant narrative, it does not necessarily translate into reality as we reach the narrative zone of the Dialogue Box. The stronger a narrative is, the less room it allows for counter-narratives, and vice versa. The determination of which is the stronger narrative will depend on how you have managed telling the corporate story, and this is where the Dialogue Box can help you to succeed through dialogue.

The Dialogue Box: Focus on narrative

FIGURE 8.1 The Dialogue Box: Focus on narrative

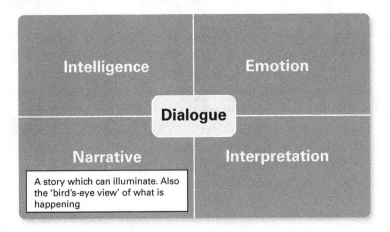

Telling the corporate story

Like the famous story from World War I, there can be a miscommunication of story elements, either intentionally or by accident. The war story goes that a message was sent by relay from the trenches back to HQ. The message was: 'Send reinforcements. We're going to advance.' By the time it reached HQ it had mutated into: 'Send three and four pence. We're going to a dance.' Perhaps apocryphal, it illustrates how a communication can change through transfer and interpretation. There may be good reason for this happening, and there can be missing story elements that change the nature of the story either deliberately or through error. In an organization, the communication process is like the game of telephones amplified, because as we have seen, there are many stories in the company as events happen and people act. These stories are told; they circulate. Many of these stories may be very humdrum, but they are continually circulating in a company or organization. Some are trivial and some are important. The important stories can be about fellow employees and the amazing things they are doing that can go unnoticed.

These stories circulate through oral transmission, and for the most part that is where they stay. These stories circulating within the organization can become part of the set of stories that explain life in the company, the kind of 'this is how we do things around here' stories. Likewise, they can become competing story versions that explain why things are not right in the organization. These things have been discussed, but there is another step and it is the major one of how these stories can thus become either authorized or accepted versions. The authorized version is the one that fits with the narrative the organization has either provided or reacts to with an acceptance or approval. However, in a difficult organizational setting this authorized version may not be the accepted version, as employees embrace other versions, such as the competing counter-narratives. In a healthy organizational setting the circulating stories can become a consistent set of stories, illuminating the corporate or organizational story in which all employees share and delight.

How then do these stories circulate? As we saw in the opening chapter, in any organization there are many natural communicators, and in oral transmission, stories are transmitted on average to some 30 people. Some communicators will be far more communicative, others less so. The important task is to find out who these 'natural communicators' in your organization are, and how to work them to help promote engagement. Before we can embark on such an exercise, we need to understand a little more about the narrative into which their stories and conversations feed.

The corporate or organization story is defined by a grand narrative, which is the dominant story or narrative that is told about the company or organization. Grand narratives are powerful and can validate or trump the message of many statements offered by the leadership. These grand narratives may comprise story lines such as:

✤ 'This is a bad/good company.'

✤ 'We have problems/opportunities.'

✤ 'Revolving doors, you know what I mean?'

✤ 'Our people are the best!'

New stories, people and events will be measured against this powerful narrative. For example, let us take a company that runs into a negative impact problem. This means as a 'bad company' it was inevitable or resulted from incompetence. As a 'good company', the problem is a blip or will be sorted out by good management. When a few people leave the organization at the same time we find that in a healthy organization it is seen as just coincidence, while in a low-morale place it is seen as further evidence of revolving doors.

So let's return to our established point that there are many communicators in your organization. The fact is we are all storytellers, some of us better than others. A good story can take us on an adventure, while a poor story leaves us cold. A good story inspires; a poor story makes us turn away. What good storytellers do is to draw us into a world of discovery, where we embark on a journey into the unknown. In this world we discover characters and events, which in turn tell us something about ourselves. In discovering other people and places we discover something about ourselves or a friend, a colleague, our organization. Whatever the story is about, there is a revelation.

In telling the story we must respect our audience. We are inviting them in, which is not achieved by insulting them, their friends or their culture. This is not to say we cannot be challenging in our story-telling. Some of the most effective stories reveal something about ourselves that is less than desirable, but in revealing this we see our need to change. The story needs to be authentic, and have a rhythm that reflects the ups and downs, threats and achievements, and other ranges of emotions and results that make the story seem real and tested. If we structure our narrative so that we only allow for the positive or motivational stories then we end up devaluing the narrative elements. People take the elements less seriously. We thrive on conflict and contrast. Every good tragic drama has moments of comedy, and every good comedy has moments of seriousness or tragedy. These contrasts draw us in, but they also reflect real life.

Getting the narrative right

This aspect of the Dialogue Box has proven the trickiest in use for Dialogue Box workshop participants. I have conducted workshops all over the world, from Shanghai and Seoul to Riyadh and Houston, and wherever I go, transitioning from the first three zones to this one is a challenge. The reason is quite simple. In the intelligence, emotion and interpretation zones we have been essentially inputting data. It takes time to draw all the data and much discussion to ensure the right details are in the right zone. However, in the narrative zone we are tying all this together to give a bird's-eye view of the situation. We are looking objectively at the data to give an honest portrait of the organization. If we discover a narrative that is close to the inherent narrative in the intelligence zone then there is no problem, no disconnect. If this is the case then probably there was no need to do a Dialogue Box in the first place, which is unlikely because the reason for doing the exercise is that there is a concern of some nature. The other reason is there is a deficiency of objectivity. I find two common errors at this stage. One is that there is wishful thinking, where the participants say what they or the management would love to hear, which again contradicts the fact there is a problem. The other common error is to write the narrative that participants would use to fix the situation, in other words write a press release or spin the problem. This is an error because it precludes dialogue to solve the situation, instead of being an honest basis on which to problem solve. So, how do we create the narrative that works?

Think of yourself as a journalist for a moment. You have done your research and spoken to various participants, and now you need to write the story from the outsider point of view. This is an important aspect of the mindset, to be critical and distanced from the data so you can find an objective measure of all the data. You need to arrange your narrative into three statements:

1 What is the SITUATION that has arisen? This is largely based on how you frame the intelligence zone. So, it may be, for instance, that Company X has launched a new initiative the management says will do Y.

2 But, and it usually is a but because we have a problem, the IMPACT is A and B. In other words, here you want to frame the emotional and interpretive response to the problem.

3 Then we state the 'SO WHAT?' factor. This is the critical part. What is the real danger in the situation? We need to have a dialogue for this reason and address the heart of the disconnect between Point 1 and Point 2. We may state if Company X does not address

A and B then there will be a decrease in morale and loss of productivity, for example.

By understanding the emotions, interpretations and stories in your organization, you will discover the narrative basis on which to engage your people, get them thinking not just about the story in itself but how it applies to them and how it affects their perception of themselves and others. Narrative that 'talks at' people creates only silence, yet it is so often what organizations and leaders do in their communications work. They become the ultimate bore at the party, except this bore has influence; they are the boss. You can leave the party, but leaving your job to escape the boredom is harder. This organizational boredom frames how so often organizations communicate by only wanting to tell the positive stories, and hide from the bad ones. They talk at employees, rather than engaging them imaginatively. The new organization, the one that will sustain the future in the 21st century, is the organization that understands these two points. By understanding the first point, you gain credibility in the way you communicate. By understanding the second point, you draw employees into your organizational story. You can draw employees in by engaging in an open narrative, in other words a dialogue. Dialogue allows you to discover the truth together, while closed narrative attempts to make you accept another's truth. What we can strive for is open dialogue, the give and take of engagement, and it is to dialogue we now turn.

Questions

1 What would you say is your current organizational narrative? Provide an objective bird's-eye view of the organization, and then compare this narrative with the narrative that is common to messages from the leadership or in articles, annual reports and other internally produced sources.

2 How does the company narrative compare to what you read in external sources, or what you hear from people in your neighbourhood or competitors?

3 Look at some recent events and break them down into the narrative elements discussed in the chapter. How far can you break down the events into a narrative, and can you compare the leadership

narrative with the narrative you were following? Can you detect a counter-narrative?

4   Is the organizational narrative a dominant narrative? What do you think can be done to strengthen the current narrative? If there are strong counter-narratives, how do you think these should be addressed?

5   What do you see as the time horizon of the organizational narrative? Is there a sense of the trajectory of the narrative in the medium and long term? How could you build the narrative to help your colleagues and employees to imagine the future, and their place in that common future?

09

The end zone: Ensuring effective dialogue – how organizations and people talk

To address internal and cultural challenges, we need to take the four zones of the Dialogue Box discussed in the last four chapters and use them to focus our dialogue, which is the end zone. If finding the right narrative proves tricky, workshop participants find choosing the dialogue word near impossible! However, it is not, and the more effective you have been in your work in the Dialogue Box so far, and the more accurate our narrative, the easier it will be to figure out the dialogue word. The objective is to ensure that we are having the right kind of dialogue, because in many situations, especially emotional ones, we can lose focus very rapidly and find everyone is settling into entrenched positions that cause confrontation rather than foster engagement. Understanding the individual elements discussed in the last four chapters will help us to focus dialogue to achieve three outcomes:

✚ First, it allows us to focus our dialogue on achieving results, drawing on the varieties of emotions, interpretations and narratives that exist within the organization.

✛ Second, it helps us to prepare for engagement, but also provides a neutral tool for various parties to have constructive, productive and engaging dialogue.

✛ Third, it provides a tool for ongoing dialogue and reiterative dialogue. The idea of the Dialogue Box is that you keep revising what you put into the zones as the situation or challenges change.

Employee engagement has become a popular theme in very recent years, and it is important to embrace dialogue as the act that is at the heart of engagement. We can only engage through dialogue, not through sending 'nice' messages or simply offering new transparency levels. What is happening in such engagement is the creation of space through dialogue, a space for negotiating differences. This process is not easy, and we have to be prepared for difficult dialogue and conversations. Leadership can often shy away from difficult conversations, but doing this creates barriers to dialogue.

What is dialogue?

To get the most basic thing out of the way first, it should be said that dialogue is not simply talk and sharing of ideas, although this is a critical part of having a dialogue (see Figure 9.1 on page 181). Talking and sharing are essentially the building blocks of a dialogue that creates new insights and understanding, which should be part of the objective of engaging dialogue. We can use dialogue to see the other person's point of view, and to refine our understanding or grasp of alternative points of view or the perceptions of our own points. Hence, dialogue is the opportunity for encounter. The reason why dialogue, especially face to face, is so important is that it is an encounter that gives us the opportunity to assess the emotions of our dialogue partner. If emotions, as we saw in the emotion zone, are capable of taking over the intelligence zone, then we should be aware that in dialogue someone may be arguing emotionally and this may be a barrier to reaching an understanding. This is something we can explore through dialogue, which is not achieved effectively in simple e-mails or even phone calls.

In dialogue we are experiencing dynamic narratives, because we are in the process of influencing or responding to the narrative, helping to shape the outcome. We have seen already how fluid narratives are, and it is the energy from this fluidity that we are trying to capture in the dialogue zone. The end game has not yet come about; there has been no final narrative, which is what we want to strive for in having a successful dialogue. We can shape a final narrative through stories connecting in relationships between parties to the dialogue. The stories we tell are relational stories, because the direct encounter of dialogue is connecting and strengthening existing relationships, or forging new ones. Hence, not only are we describing the world, the modus operandi of 20th-century communications, but we are also changing the world. We can invite our dialogue partners to engage with us to make change, which is obviously not as easy as it sounds. Sometimes it takes one side to take the initiative or to take the first step towards the middle ground, and if you're reading this book closely then you know this needs to be you! The first step can be the invitation to dialogue, and you're in a good position to do this. Additionally, the step is taken in recognition that there is some flexibility on your side, a possibility that there may be another way or refinement to your approach that will achieve the same result. In dialogue we have the opportunity for correctives, where we can correct mistakes or misperceptions, or at least to set out our position clearly even if it is not initially accepted by our dialogue partners.

The flipside of invitation to dialogue is silence or blame. Naturally dialogue cannot take place if only one side is talking, but often the next step on is the blame game. To create engaging dialogue we need to ensure we avoid dialogue as blame, using any encounter to score points or blaming the other side for what is going wrong, as this would not be a corrective exercise but a destructive one. When we get into the blame game we know things will only deteriorate as people dig into their entrenched positions. Such dialogue has a predictable trajectory – we know this.

In fact, each dialogue we have has a trajectory, and we can project forward to assess what the arc of that trajectory can be. The trouble is that often we lose sight of the dialogue, and so the interaction loses focus and direction. At this point we want to look for dialogue correctives, things that will get the conversation and interaction back on course. This is why we need to avoid dialogue becoming a blame game, a way of finding who is at fault when there is a problem. This does not mean we are looking to deflect criticism or accountability; if there are concerns then they need to be part of the conversation. If we conduct dialogue as a mutual engagement then it is possible to clarify the concerns and differences participating parties have, and make sure we at least understand where the other party stands and how they are understanding us. When we do this we create new space through dialogue, because we have started to figure out where the gaps exist between parties and viewpoints. When we do this we also have to acknowledge that dialogue can be difficult, and that the assumptions we may be making are out in the open, and they may be left wanting. By realizing that dialogue has a trajectory, we can map out where we think the conversation will go, because we look more closely at our assumptions and how they might be interpreted by other parties.

Opposite this open dialogue are the dialogue inhibitors, and ways in which the trajectory of a dialogue can be blocked or redirected. It is critical we are aware of these and whether they are present in the situations we face. A major inhibitor of open dialogue is fear. The leadership, by virtue of their positions, create a certain level of fear, but they can also create greater fear by being unapproachable or by having lots of gatekeepers between them and the employee. Often a leader will say, 'I have an open door policy', but this does not mean people will feel free to walk through the door or that the leadership's gatekeepers will allow anyone through. There are, of course, some good reasons for this, such as scheduling needs and privacy. However, these are short term, and priorities may be justifiably changed in situations where an open door to dialogue is critical.

There are many other types of blockers or inhibitors to mention. These include uncertainty, where someone is uncertain of their own position to comment or unsure about the information they have available. People may have low confidence or self-esteem, which stops them from opening up a dialogue. There may be environmental factors, such as a busy office, the existence of gatekeepers or an open-plan office where everyone can see who you're talking to, making people reticent to open up dialogue. There may also be concerns related to other dialogue partners, and who has the competency or position to speak. The presence of one dialogue partner may inhibit another from speaking, perhaps due to status or being new to the dialogue or organization. As a result, someone may not be participating in dialogue or speaking, not because they don't want to, but because various factors are militating against them doing so, in which case we need to be aware of these factors and find ways to open dialogue and connect.

Fostering dialogue

In dialogue we are connecting to self and others. The second part may appear obvious to you, but the first may puzzle slightly. The difficulty for all of us at times is that we become disconnected, even from ourselves. We can get stuck in a groove or a rut of understanding. We become so used to looking at someone or something in a particular way that we lose touch with our own feelings about the person or the thing, or we simply lose perspective. When we look at situations, we hear people say, 'How could you have done something so stupid!' If we do something wrong or make a mistake, it can happen because we have disconnected in some way. Leadership can do this when they surround themselves with 'yes men', and exclude different or opposing views. When this happens the viewpoint gets stuck in a rut. It may seem like, or be defended as, being certain or right or consistent. But what if it's wrong? A little humility is an important ingredient to good dialogue. Always being open to dialogue challenges helps to refine the plan or the idea, as commonly plans and ideas are malleable. We may be confident in our dialogue position and the intelligence we possess, but there can be a fine line between obstinacy and certainty. We can be certain using a working hypothesis, but as John Maynard Keynes said, when the facts change we can change our minds, and we always have to be open to the impact of changing facts. The appearance of new facts or challenging points of view can provide us with clarity, allowing us to strengthen our plan or idea because that is what is important, not the interests of those seeking to impact the plan or idea. Hence, our position is one of continually seeking understanding.

In cases where there is no dialogue or dialogue is being hindered or prevented altogether, it is important to be able to locate any blockers, as discussed in the previous section, but also to find ways to foster dialogue. This can be habitual, and you may be doing this already, but it is worth just reflecting on this for a moment. Formal meetings are an important opportunity for dialogue, but they can be managed to ensure that greater dialogue is achieved by using simple dialogue devices. When meetings start, and even when someone joins the meeting late, people get more productive by virtue of having been introduced. This means that starting a meeting by introducing people can already get things moving along, because you are establishing who does what and where they fit, allowing each participant to build dialogue partners into their own mind map of the meeting. By having people introduce themselves, you are getting something very basic done: you are getting them to speak their first words, and this makes it easier to join in the conversation. When someone starts a meeting silent, the longer the meeting goes on the harder it is for them to start talking. Naturally, there are many people who have no such problem, who speak freely or only when they have something to say. The point is that you are providing the basis for accommodating a variety of comfort zones.

In making sure we connect people we are doing something else. By listening to others and entertaining new ideas, we are in fact recognizing values. There are other people and ideas that have value in the world, and we can find ways through dialogue to try to accommodate these other values, both to respect different values and to see how they can have a positive impact on our own values. In our diverse and globalized world, this is becoming increasingly more important and more challenging. It is important that we see that people from other places, whether it is within the organization or on the other side of the world, have a value and a contribution to make to the ideas and plans the organization is pursuing. This is both a respectful and a creative way forward. In one sense this means accepting we don't have all the answers, but it also invites others to connect with us in the expectation that they have a contribution to make. In this way, the question of dialogue becomes a fundamental one to ask yourself: are you willing to be in dialogue to connect to others and to meet in a process of mutual discovery? This immediately creates an egalitarian ideal, which can be problematic because all organizations have rules and governance, and they are in part sustained by power and may be challenged by the 'openness' of dialogue. However, being open in the opportunities for dialogue does not mean you cannot keep structures, processes and formalities in place; it is simply using them in such a way as to foster effective dialogue.

In connecting we recognize there is the question of status, because organizations have structure, protocols and hierarchies. This can give rise to various conditions of status envy and anxiety, the organizational equivalent of 'keeping up with the Joneses'. There is, I venture, a big future in how we assess and implement authority and hierarchy in organizations, as we seek to flatter organizations and people seek more level playing fields. I won't attempt to answer this here, though I believe the Dialogue Box is a big step to moving more productively in this direction. This can lead to interesting conversations about whether we are communicating to levels or people as individuals. To illustrate, we can try to communicate to ambitious people in an organization, or we can communicate to levels as representative of ambition. However, we may be including or excluding individuals who do not truly meet our criteria. Hence, an individual can be full of ambition but working on the shop floor, or could be in middle management biding their time – who do we want to inspire? Equally, working mothers may be on the shop floor or in the C-Suite and have things in common, or respond to certain messages, because of their roles outside of the organization. There is much scope for research in seeing how this will impact internal communications beyond the scope of this book, but dialogue will play a role in many discussions that will help organizations to reach any conclusions.

The roles that people play in the organization are also changing in terms of the authority placed in the role and how they are perceived by the internal audience. If we look at the role of the leadership, we can ask whether such a role is viewed, to use a sporting comparison, as one of the most senior managers, as a player/manager or as a team captain. Different leaders will play the role differently: some will be more autocratic than others, while some will be more coaching in their approach. The best leaders probably have to be a mixture: someone who can coach team members to improve and deliver, while prepared to take difficult decisions and just get the job done. Just as we are changing the way we communicate to internal audiences, we may see changes in how leadership functions. We already have in a generation. Where there was the 'boss' and the 'employee' and an authority of command, we now see a much more cooperative and consensual model of management. Again, this is an area of further research, but it would not surprise me if we moved to a dynamic organizational model, not unlike that of a flock of geese. When geese fly in formation they have the strongest geese on the edges for aerodynamic reasons, and the less strong or rest-ing geese in the middle protected by the others. They switch places, with the stronger ones taking a rest and ones from the middle moving to the outside. When a bird is injured or needs greater rest, others will stay with them and help them catch up. When we talk of the ideal of a 'flat organization', could this be it? Perhaps we can see a case of the much-touted business survival of the fitness using Darwinism with a difference. Again, whatever evolves in terms of ideal organizational structures will be arrived at more effectively through dialogue.

These are not idle speculations on future changes, and they are important to bear in mind because change is not a smooth and pas-sive process. Dialogue will pave the way, whatever future organiza-tional models evolve, and your dialogue will help pave the way to innovate the future of organizational structure, and the more innova-tive you are in your dialogue the more innovative your solutions will be. Change for the organization means change for individuals, and different people react to change differently. If change is happening around me, and someone is offering to support me, I may ask myself whether this person, or these changes, are keeping me in my place or giving me a helping hand. We can ask whether a 'flat organization' is one without power structures, or one where status envy and anxieties are trumped by effective use of responsibility and skill levels. Dia-logue will help ensure these concerns and opportunities are addressed effectively and in a supportive manner, rather than delivered down from up high. Any solution – no matter how good – if simply deliv-ered, without consultation and dialogue, will attract problems, caused by the process itself. Many decisions are taken on the basis of what is the right thing to do, yet run into opposition because people are reacting against the means of delivery. Office changes are among the most common, where an intelligent and efficient model may be designed for a new office or reorganization of existing space, but is then delivered fait accompli and with disastrous outcomes.

Connecting and disconnecting

In dialogue we aim to communicate to connect, and we do this by using phrases and terms that include people and connect us to them. The following are some of the phrases we can use that connect us and invite others to join with us in the dialogue and actions that will advance the organization:

- Us, we, all…
- How can we do this together?
- I made a mistake; how can I fix this?
- Can you help me?
- You did a great job!
- I appreciate what you did.
- You've made this a better project.
- Let's do this again!

Of course, there are ways to do just the opposite, ways in which we communicate to disconnect, and here are some examples of how we use dialogue that disconnects us:

- Me, myself and I…
- I did this.
- My team did well.
- This is my problem.
- Go away!
- Silence.
- Jargon.
- Insider narrative.

Observe how the first six points are ways in which we verbally or visually set ourselves apart from others, setting us above others and keeping others in their place. The other two are examples of how we do this verbally to exclude others, and I want to discuss these a little more here.

Jargon and insider narrative are both double-edged swords. For example, an engineer will use jargon as a form of shorthand and to be precise, or to ensure that the other engineer knows what is being talked about and has the correct level of understanding to do the job. The education of an engineer involves many levels of sophistication, and the higher up, the more jargon there is that a novice has yet to learn. This is a positive and important use of jargon. However, the opposite can be achieved, by using jargon to shut someone out or to make someone look foolish because they don't understand. We can use insider narrative in the same way. This involves talking about people or places that one or more persons present have no knowledge of, so they do not get the references, jokes and so on. This can again be a form of shorthand. However, insider narrative can also be used to let someone know they do not have full membership rights to the group. In both cases, with jargon and insider narrative, in constructive dialogue there are subtle ways to include someone, by explaining a term in such a way that the newcomer is connected or briefly noting who a person is in the story being told. In this way, we are connecting people, drawing them in and making them feel part of the conversation, part of the group.

Disconnected intelligence

The notion of dialogue disconnecting is not simply to encourage everyone to be 'nice' and 'inclusive' rather than disconnecting people. We can use dialogue to connect with intelligence, and there are a number of threats to an organization when intelligence is disconnected, and where we find there is a blockage of knowledge. Having dialogue does not need to be constrained to a single issue or strategy; it can feed into the bigger picture. Most companies have some kind of knowledge management strategy, and dialogue should be part of this, along with the internal communications function. The reason is that dialogue leads to deeper knowledge and intelligence in individuals and organizations. When involved in dialogue we are both informing and being informed by the dialogue taking place, thereby creating new insights and knowledge.

However, we can find that gaining insights and knowledge is hampered by the problem that the discernment of the known is eclipsed by the unknowns. Let me explain. A little while ago I met Donald

Rumsfeld, and I was reminded of his famous saying: 'There are known knowns. These are things we know that we know. There are known unknowns. That is to say, there are things that we now know we don't know. But there are also unknown unknowns. These are things we do not know we don't know.' He was ridiculed for saying this, and the whole idea of 'knowns' and 'unknowns' entered into the language of political and cultural humour. Yet let's break down what he said. There are:

- ❖ known knowns – things we know we know;
- ❖ subtlety – things we now know we don't know about; and
- ❖ unknown unknowns – things we do not know.

If we apply this to our organization, we can say the following:

- ❖ There are things we do know about our organization, our strategy, competition and the like. We know we know them, and we make use of these things.

- ❖ As events change, things come into view that we realize, or know, we do not know. I can know that I do not know the feelings of employees about a decision, for instance.

- ❖ Then there are things I do not know that I do not know; these are the real surprises in life.

I don't wish to labour this point, but in the midst of writing his speech this all seemed to make sense to Mr Rumsfeld and his advisers, and if you break it down you can see what he intended to say. However, once put into the soundbite media space it all of a sudden falls apart and he is ridiculed. It takes on a life of its own. This was, for Rumsfeld, no doubt an unknown unknown. The danger of dialogue is that we may say what we do not intend to say, or what we say can get distorted by the medium of communication. In the television and internet age there is less room for subtlety and sophistication. As the famous Canadian communications expert Marshall McLuhan said, 'The medium is the message.' On hearing this, American comedian Ernie Kovacs quipped that television is the medium because it is neither rare nor well done; banter, as today's younger generation would say.

In making connections, dialogue presupposes that we often have insufficient knowledge, and so we engage with others to test our assumptions, to connect and find new knowledge. There are, however, barriers to connecting knowledge that we need to overcome through dialogue. We may find ourselves in a position where we are unable to systematize to make sense of events, and dialogue can share insights that help us to understand events. We may have a diminished capacity to be objective, because we are too close to someone or an event, and so dialogue can help us to stand back, find the objective view and focus our attention better. There are times when people and events will challenge the understood ethical norms of an organization, and dialogue can help to assess the validity of the norms or correct the situation. There are also barriers that make it hard for us to appraise events, such as key events not occurring, validity of key information not being established, or the pathway to understanding not being ready because we are taken by surprise or are simply unprepared.

This interaction in relationships through dialogue helps us to form new knowledge. The illumination produces new knowledge and causes us to act, as we rarely keep things to ourselves and tend to pass on illuminating stories, or at least our recollection of what we are told. In this way knowledge is passed on and circulated, though the quality of knowledge will vary greatly from the trivial or benign through to great insights and important connections. This storytelling form of illumination produces new knowledge because we connect the insights of one narrative to shine a light on other narratives we have in mind, or we connect hitherto separate events into a new coherent narrative.

Disconnected emotions

When emotions are disconnected we can find that there is a creation of new priorities or a re-arrangement of existing priorities, as we discussed in Chapter 6. The intelligent work is done, but then the emotional impact is such that other things, often seemingly trivial, impact on the situation. This is partly because in the intelligence phases we focus on rational behaviour, but of course behaviour can be quite irrational. However, it is more than this. The emotions can bring certain aspects into focus, which may or may not be where the focus needs to be. The emotions can go further and distort the reality of the situation, fed by rumours and conspiracy theories. There is a whole array of possibilities. Hence, in a situation where there is a reorganization, the primary emotions of uncertainty and loss of colleagues can combine to create fear amongst those who are 'safe' that they are in peril of losing their jobs as well.

On a more mundane level, but just as critical to the well-being of the organization, emotions in the life of an individual or amongst a group can cause physiological changes that impact the work of individuals and organizations; for example, tiredness resulting in actions such as rumour, absenteeism and decreased work rates. When we see these symptoms in the workplace they may just be that, symptoms of a problem elsewhere rather than an individual behaving badly at work. Dialogue can be used to explore these difficulties, establish what the problem is and open pathways to solving it.

Dialogue is also a means to stabilize a situation, and again can be a double-edged sword. In managing our emotions we can use dialogue to seek affirmation from others to stabilize our sense of an event. In other words, we talk to others to calibrate our understanding of people or events, which can be a self-fulfilling exercise of seeking out narratives that affirm what we already suspect or believe in order to embed our own sense of narrative. More positively though, we can undertake the same exercise to verify the facts or test out our assumptions, and come to the conclusion that we have not grasped the truth of the situation or have only a partial grasp. Dialogue in these circumstances helps us to come to a full understanding, but only because we have been prepared to change course, even if in the end we do not have to change.

Disconnected interpretation

When interpretation is disconnected we will find the event or person we are trying to understand is in a very fluid state. The facts may well be one thing, but there are various interpretations circulating as to what the facts mean or contradicting specific aspects. On one level this means that prior understanding and assumptions remain unchallenged by changing events. As the saying goes, people see what they want to see and interpret the facts to fit such prior assumptions. New information gets tested against the interpretation and the credibility of new interpretive statements gains a stronghold, and so the interpretation builds on new events to reinforce or entrench the position. This means that divining the truth of statements and events is hampered, and other parties to the dialogue need to be able to understand this and find ways to dislodge the interpretations. The reason for this explanation is that ultimately interpretations in circulation can become currency in the marketplace of organizational morale, for better or worse. These interpretations then start to feed into the narrative or counter-narrative.

Disconnected narrative

Narrative is disconnected when the narrative formulated in the intelligence zone is at odds with the accepted narrative internally, or where there are strong competing or counter-narratives. The various interpretations that have emerged are components of the overarching narratives in existence, and may form part of more than one narrative. This is what makes the narrative so difficult to judge, and why leadership may be fooled into thinking one narrative has triumphed over another. Interpretations are to narrative what smoke is to fire. We are led from the varying interpretations towards the presence of narrative. A narrative as internal storytelling emerges to illuminate events and interpretations circulating within the organization, and as the narrative is filled with more detail it can trump other narratives or be subsumed by a larger narrative. This illumination in turn produces new knowledge, which informs our relationships and how we think about the people and events involved. We start to interpret through the lens of this narrative, and so the function of interpretation changes. Narrative is the objective reading of the subjective views rehearsed in the interpretive stage. It is the stage at which we can stand back and see what is happening, where the story is leading us. As the process evolves, we seek out those who can add to our narrative, fill out the detail and fill in the gaps. This strengthens the narrative, and gives it a more objective feel. In a difficult situation, pessimism can spread as the narrative becomes more coherent, even though it is not necessarily true.

If we are in such a difficult situation then we need to reconnect through dialogue. This means looking at your communications as dialogic, a term drawn from literary criticism that refers to literary works in dialogue with other works and thus informing and being informed by other works of literature. In our dialogue context, this means that the dialogue we have informs and is informed by other dialogue partners. This process creates dynamic narratives that help us to shape the narratives of participants to the dialogue and allow our dialogue in turn to be shaped by others in a two-way process. This makes relational stories of paramount importance, as we are looking to build relationships in this dialogic process. The exciting prospect for our dialogue is that we are not just describing but changing the world.

Dialogue takes place in different environments, but for our purposes it is useful to outline four key categories:

✤ formal;

✤ business;

✤ informal; and

✤ fun stuff.

Formal dialogue takes place in a very structured way, and there is a high degree of awareness regarding roles and positions, the use of language and the presence of distancing body language. This can be so in a variety of social and business settings. We all take part in formal communication, perhaps at a social event, in a meeting with a bank manager asking for a loan or being introduced to a dignitary. This formal setting overlaps with business, where rules of conduct and behaviour are constrained to a greater or lesser extent, depending on the business. Media companies tend to be rather less formal than bankers, but each still abides by a degree of formality. Then we have informal dialogue, which also overlaps with business, because we will be friendly and informal with colleagues, bosses and customers. Our social relationships outside of work are usually very informal. Finally, we have the fun stuff! Our social relationships are often highlighted by doing fun stuff together, going to parties, sports events and other places. However, business can have fun stuff as well, particularly at conferences, the Christmas party, family days and so on. As noted, these categories overlap and interact, but it does lead us to see there are more dimensions at the workplace than we may be paying attention to, and to connect we need to be more aware of these channels.

Losing community: things not to do

❖ Don't keep people in the dark.

❖ Don't spin or obfuscate.

❖ Don't forget the isolated.

❖ Don't neglect feedback.

❖ Don't panic!

Creating a community at work: things to do

❖ Engage and involve.

❖ Inspire an open and transparent culture.

❖ Encourage and value feedback.

❖ Utilize all relevant communications channels.

❖ Explain change.

❖ Project and protect the brand internally.

❖ Be consistent.

❖ Create role models.

❖ Live the message.

❖ Train and develop talent.

❖ Research and assess external perceptions.

❖ Have a clear statement of objectives.

❖ Be clear on principles underpinning your strategy.

- ✤ Contextualize your messages.

- ✤ Be clear about your target audiences.

- ✤ Use preferred channels of your audiences.

- ✤ Establish working project plans, deadlines and responsibilities.

- ✤ Get your timing right.

- ✤ Build in evaluation measures.

- ✤ Develop an annual communications plan.

The Dialogue Box ready for use

FIGURE 9.1   The Dialogue Box ready for use

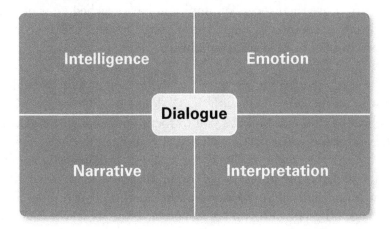

Working with your dialogue word

In workshops, participants enjoy the challenge of finding the right word, but they often think I know the answer as I strike out their many attempts to arrive at the word. The important point here is to know we are discovering the word together, there is no pre-set answer. All the words that are offered by participants in this exercise are useful and may be useful to create a vocabulary for the various communications needed to engage in dialogue, because they form a set of words that resonate with the narrative and your dialogue partners. However, what you are looking for is that one special word that will help you do the following:

- prepare you for dialogue;
- set the tone of voice for your dialogue;
- help you define your messaging;
- be your compass to navigate your engagement;
- be consistent by creating a test word for all your communications.

However, like having fish or relatives in your house, the word has a life expectancy! In some cases, the word will only be used once, having done the job and moved the dialogue on. In other cases, the word may be around for some time doing its work. As soon as the zones of the Dialogue Box are changed then the dialogue word needs to change to move the process on until you have reached your destination. Your destination is when the intelligence and narrative zones are reconnected or reflect one another.

At one level, the search for the word is important as it provides a focus for all the work done with the Dialogue Box. On another level, searching for the word allows you to focus your dialogue and when found, the word will reflect the clarity of your narrative and point the way towards the solution. This is not to say that finding the word is a magic bullet; it is the start of your communications work using all the channels and skills at your disposal. The question that is often asked at this point is, 'How do you know you have the right word?' This is not a science, it is an art, and you'll know when you try the word out and see how it fits with the situation. Once you have this word it will drive your communication; it is not the communication itself, though you will usually use the word.

To help you in locating the word, there are a few more guidelines that can help you:

- First of all, it isn't easy!
- You only need one word! It gives focus, clarity and allows you to capture the essence of what you need to communicate.

❖ The word needs to resonate and connect emotionally.

❖ It should have impact.

❖ It should be result-orientated.

❖ It can be a positive or a negative word.

❖ It all depends on the context and the target audience.

There are other guidelines to help you (see box below), but this part of the Dialogue Box is where you truly come to terms with all the work you have done in the other zones. It will force you to re-examine your assumptions, figure out your audience and what they think and feel, and drive you toward a more meaningful dialogue. Once you have found your dialogue word then you are ready to use all the traditional communications tools at your disposal and to meet your audience.

Testing your dialogue word

To help you decide on your dialogue word there are some tests you can use to see if you have found the right word. Your word should:

❖ Inspire others to listen to you – would you listen to you?

❖ Create a neutral space – your word should not be self-serving.

❖ Encourage a connection – the word may mean different things to you and dialogue partners yet still connect you.

❖ Avoid common management speak – people tune out to buzz terms and jargon.

❖ Work from top management to the shop floor – is it an easy word?

❖ Resonate with emotion – will people feel your word?

❖ Work it in a sentence – does it appeal emotionally to you?

❖ Fit many contexts – it is very adaptable and supports you.

❖ Have some presence in your analysis already – do you see it in the emotion zone?

❖ Lead into using other words in your new vocabulary – all your words are useful!

Epilogue

In concluding this work I have not used the heading 'conclusion', instead opting for 'epilogue'. This is because dramatic narratives have epilogues rather than conclusions and I have aspired in this book to offer you a dramatic approach to internal communication based on dialogue. As you work your way through applying this dialogue approach to your organization, you can ask whether there is a new paradigm in view for your organization and the way in which you engage with your employees through internal communications. You can also ask of your organization an even bigger question, one that goes to the heart of how you understand your organization: Is this a place of work or a community at work, working for each other? I hope that this book can play an instrumental role in creating new and dynamic dialogue within your organization, and help you to take major steps towards being a true community at work.

Questions

You will be working with the Dialogue Box to piece all the elements together, so we will not go into real examples in these questions. What we can ask are the following three fundamental questions before you go into the workshop section of the book:

1   Is your organization open to dialogue with employees?
2   To what depth do you think leadership is prepared to go, and how honest a dialogue do you think your organization is capable of having?
3   Are you ready to explore dialogue in your organization?

10

Using the Dialogue Box

1. Explaining the Dialogue Box

This section of the book is a practical workshop-type set of exercises to help you make use of the Dialogue Box, either in an individual setting or as a group session. It does this in four sections:

✤ Using the Dialogue Box before an event.

✤ Using the Dialogue Box after an event.

✤ Using a Dialogue Box exercise.

✤ Using the Dialogue Box in your organization.

These sections will take you step by step through the thinking process, using the Dialogue Box in a practical way. While there is a lot of theory behind the Dialogue Box, it is not a theoretical tool. It is very much a practical tool. To help you, the first section is an overview of the Dialogue Box based on the main chapters of this book, providing you with some points to reflect on individually or work through as a group. The next two sections will lead you through two examples based on real-world cases. These are based on a combination of real cases to protect the identity of the original cases. The third and final section will allow you to start applying the Dialogue Box within your own organization, firstly by doing an exercise based on your past experience with another organization, and then an exercise to address a situation in your current position.

This short re-introduction is simply to highlight some of the points to hold in the forefront of your mind about the zones in the Dialogue Box and to use practically when making use of the Dialogue Box either individually or in a group session. You will have read the in-depth discussion of the zones of the Dialogue Box, with some of the theoretical background, so these points are distilled here for ease of use and the slides may be used in group sessions to guide your discussion.

Now is the time to dive in and use the Dialogue Box!

As we have seen, there are five zones to the Dialogue Box:

1 Intelligence.

2 Emotion.

3 Interpretation.

4 Narrative.

5 Dialogue.

If you are unclear on any points in the material that follows then go back to the relevant chapter and revise the material therein. Let's go through each of the elements of the Dialogue Box step by step, starting with intelligence.

Intelligence

This is about the rationale and reasoning behind any decision, action or project that you might present to your internal audience. In using the Dialogue Box, you need not agree with the decision or even like it! The point is to identify that this is what has been decided, and your job is to figure out how to communicate internally in the most effective way. Look at Figure 10.1 and be clear as to what we mean by intelligence. If you are in a group session, hold a discussion on what people mean by intelligence and make sure you are all talking about the same thing.

FIGURE 10.1 Intelligence

> **Intelligence**
>
> • Rational and reasoning
> • Discernment of the known and unknowns
> • Capacity for knowledge
> • Systematizing to make sense
> • Capacity to be objective
> • Capacity to act ethically
> • Individual and group intelligence

Figure 10.1 highlights the points discussed in the chapter, and draws our attention toward the things we do when we are using our intelligence, making sense of our data and planning our steps, as well as making judgements about right and wrong or distinguishing our personal views from what is best in the situation. Note we can be talking about the intelligence at either an individual or collective level. This is important to note, because often a group is guided by what becomes the shared rationale as individuals get behind the rationale, on occasion resulting in the group going in the wrong direction!

In a nutshell: the Dialogue Box makes no assumption about whether the intelligence is good or bad, since often that is subjective. The point is to look at engagement once you have decided to do something. If this something is unpopular, for example, then the Dialogue Box will help you to engage with employees to get the calmest possible outcome. Going through the Dialogue Box exercise predictively, you may decide to change some aspects of your intelligence based on your conclusions. Equally, using the Dialogue Box after the event may help you to locate those aspects of your intelligence that can be reinforced or changed through dialogue.

Emotion

Emotion can easily override intelligence, and is the number one culprit when communication goes wrong. Remember how often you have fired off an e-mail in anger or had to hold yourself back from doing so. Recall how emotional you felt about something personal, perhaps your performance or something you'd worked intensely on for a period of time, only to find someone simply ignoring or insulting the product of your hard work.

In your exercise select a very specific event you don't mind talking about, but one where you clearly felt emotional as events unfolded. Recall the mood you were in before the event and how that changed. What were your instinctive reactions to the people involved? How did you appraise the situation, and how did your emotions change as the event unfolded? Explain the issue and your responses, as well as those of other actors in the event. Now, write down or discuss these emotions and how they affected your actions and the outcome. This means understanding the physical and emotional changes you experienced, locating the points at which your priorities were rearranged, what factors and actions of others sparked your emotions, and, assessing how you could have handled the situation better.

In a nutshell: emotions are not to be dismissed or avoided, no matter how uncomfortable the situation may feel. It is about recognizing that employees have a stake in your organization and want to know their place in your intelligence. In good situations we want to raise the emotions, and in bad situations we want to calm the emotions. Internal communication boils down to emotional management; it is something we are trying to do most of the time with our messaging and engaging.

FIGURE 10.2 Emotion

Emotion

- Mood, motivation, instinct
- Primary emotions combine (fear, anger, sadness, joy)
- Intelligent appraisal, physiological change, action
- Create or re-arrange priorities
- Emotions revealed physically
- Managing our emotions and emotions of others

Interpretation

Take a specific event you recall when there was a range of opinion about what happened. Note down the interpretation you had, but also the other interpretations that people told you they had of the event. These do not need to all be radically different; they just need to have a variance with other interpretations.

We interpret subjectively and objectively. The technical terms for these two types of interpretation are eisegetical and exegetical. In the former case, we read what we want into the situation; in the latter, we try to understand the situation from a distance. We do this all the time, often changing from one form to the other according to the situation or our emotional state. Can you recall situations where you have looked very subjectively and objectively? How did this turn out?

What you are looking for in these various interpretations is how people have looked subjectively at events, depending on their position, personality, relationships, etc. What someone says may reveal or conceal something about themselves or the situation, and when confronted with various interpretations of the same event we have a natural inclination to search for and understand the truth of what is being said, which may come from one person or many.

In a nutshell: you have to look objectively at the situation you are analysing and record as many interpretations as possible, some of which may seem very unpleasant or even bizarre to you! Only by

FIGURE 10.3 Interpretation

Interpretation

- Eisegetical and exegetical interpretation
- Verbal and non-verbal signs
- Prior understanding and assumptions
- Revealing or concealing?
- Divining the truth of statements and signs

entertaining all the possibilities can you get down to distilling the interpretations that are driving the narrative or counter-narrative.

Narrative

Now we come to understanding what is going on. In the intelligence zone we have an implicit narrative. It is what we want people to think of as the rationale or trajectory of a decision or event. The narrative we may find emerging from a situation, through the prism of the emotions and various interpretations floating about, may be quite different. The narrative that emerges within your organization may, in fact, turn out to be a strong counter-narrative that challenges the implied narrative in your intelligence zone.

In this zone you can explore how the stories circulating in your organization are used to illuminate a particular event or situation. You can assess what new knowledge emerges out of this narrative; does it tell us something we didn't know before? Is there a narrative that trumps your intelligence, meaning you need a dialogue that will take you back to reconsidering your actions or decisions? Or is this counter-narrative simply a compelling untruth that is trumping your intelligence, requiring you to find a dialogue route that will get your plans back on track?

Narrative, in creating knowledge, informs our relationships, and we can look at a situation or event and learn whether new knowledge undermines confidence in the relationship between management and employees, or between colleagues, and so on. In looking at narrative

FIGURE 10.4 Narrative

Narrative

- Storytelling to illuminate, produces new knowledge
- Knowledge informs our relationships
- Narrative is interpretive
- Gives less room for counter-narrative
- Telling only the positive stories devalues narrative elements
- Narrative that 'talks at' creates only silence

we are receiving an interpretation of events, so the narrative that triumphs can still be untrue or leave room for debate. The stronger a narrative is, however, the less room it gives to other narratives and the more likely it can become dominant.

In presenting your narrative of an event be sure to include the negative, because only presenting the positive side of things will be less credible. This means being realistic about your narrative when dealing with difficult situations, but it is the 'negative' elements that will be the ones persuading others of a counter-narrative, or they may be the elements that give the receiver of your narrative something to hold on to during the dialogue. The fact you admit to a wrong or a weakness is an invitation to dialogue. Your narrative also has to give scope for the receiver to engage. If the narrative only speaks at the receiver then it will soon be of less interest. Ask the question of how the receiver of your narrative fits into this narrative.

As you think through your narrative, remember there are some fixed elements in a narrative, so you can break down your exercise into defining the facts of the situation, assessing the wisdom that is accepted in the company or may arise, who the key characters are, what the situation is you are analysing and the event that everyone expects will happen or has already taken place. You can use this exercise predictively and retrospectively.

In a nutshell: how can I develop a narrative in my intelligence zone that is both compelling and engaging, and that allows less room for counter-narrative?

FIGURE 10.5 Defining the narrative elements

Narrative elements

- Facts – downsizing announcement
- Wisdom – impact on the company
- Characters – boss, employee
- Situations – meeting
- The event – rumour is employee dismissed

Dialogue

This is the zone you are trying to get to, and find the single word that will guide you through the dialogue you need to have with employees. You are looking for a word that will anchor your conversations, a word that you can keep at the forefront of your mind to keep your conversation anchored in calmness. It is also a word that is a compass to guide your dialogue and to help you through to the endpoint.

FIGURE 10.6 Finding ways to communicate empathetically

Communicating...

Empathetically

- I understand your needs.
- I can see why you are upset/offended
- I know what it feels like.
- I'm sorry
- Can we work this out?

Non-empathetically

- I'm sorry, but you've got this all wrong
- See me later
- This is my project
- You are wrong
- You're making this a bigger deal than it is

FIGURE 10.7 Looking for ways to connect

Communicating to...

Connect

- Us, we, all...
- How can we do this together?
- Can you help me?
- You did a great job!
- I appreciate what you did.
- You've made this a better project
- Let's do this again!

Disconnect

- Me, myself and I...
- I did this
- My team did well
- This is my problem
- Go away!
- Jargon
- Insider narrative
- Silence

When you communicate empathetically you use an approach that shows you understand, which need not mean that you agree with others. It is a first dialogue step, to move your position towards them or draw them towards you. It also involves recognizing what the other person thinks or feels, which will tend to open them up a little, some more quickly than others.

You can communicate to connect and disconnect with people. However, it is easy to resort to language and actions that throw up the barriers and stop dialogue, which may have their place but not usually when you are trying to foster dialogue.

Dialogue is best achieved in person. Being together we can more easily see the impact our words and actions are having on another person, and we can react to verbal and body language signals as cues

FIGURE 10.8 Defining dialogue

Dialogue

- Dialogue is not simply talk and sharing of ideas
- Dialogue is the opportunity for encounter
- Encounter assesses the emotions
- Dialogue creates new insights and understanding
- Dialogue leads to deeper knowledge/intelligence

FIGURE 10.9 Mastering empathetic dialogue

Dialogue is about empathy

- Listening
- Connecting
- Valuing the other person
- Cultivating sensitivity
- Communicating the human spirit with the action
- Sharing personal space
- Acknowledging and accepting
- Understanding your own feelings

to either push forward or back off. This is rarely achieved in e-mail, which more often results in miscommunication and electronic warfare! Dialogue is also a creative process that allows us to learn more about a situation, ourselves and others. It leads us into deeper knowledge and improves our work in the intelligence zone.

There also something inherently empathetic about dialogue. While sometimes we need 'tough talking', mostly we are trying to find a point of connection in a fractured situation. As the Leonard Cohen song says: 'There is a crack in everything, that's how the light gets in.' We are standing in that light, trying to illuminate our spirit and points of connection or agreement. This allows us to explore a situation together rather than remain in conflict or silence. We can also check our own feelings when faced with someone in dialogue. Imagine if the person we are about to fire off an angry e-mail to was standing in front of us. Would we do it? No, we behave differently when in contact with people, though admittedly sometimes someone can have the ability to really annoy us in person!

In a nutshell: what single word can you put in the dialogue zone that will guide you through your engagement with employees, and act as both your conversational anchor and as a negotiating compass?

One last, but important thing: we are looking for a single concept for each zone to define the situation, and to arrive at a single word that can go into the dialogue zone. This is the discipline you are asked to exercise in full. So, let's explore using the Dialogue Box!

FIGURE 10.10   The Dialogue Box ready for use

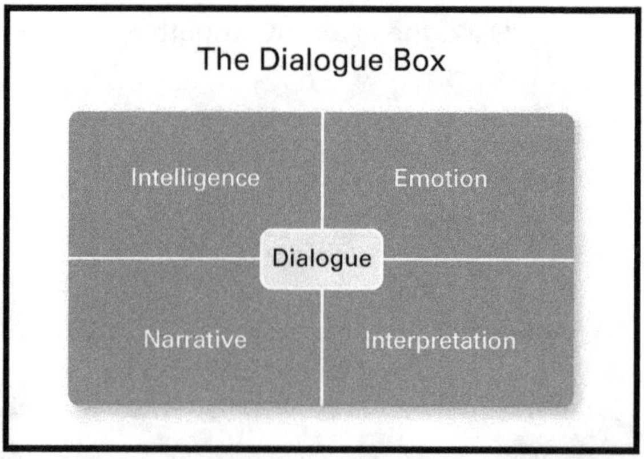

2. Using the Dialogue Box

I: Using the Dialogue Box before an event

They say there is nothing better than hindsight. Well there is now: it's called the Dialogue Box! This section will help you to think through how to plan internal communications before an announcement or event, to prepare for the angles and to minimize the room for error. It is a process of foresight, which will allow you to think through the impact any plan or decision may have on your organization so that you can anticipate the lines of dialogue that will likely result. Taking this approach will then allow you to discover what dialogue you will need to have with your internal audiences, and keep your project or decision on track. This is the ideal way to use the Dialogue Box, making use of it as a planning tool. Intuitively we can figure out the kinds of reactions that may result from a plan or decision, but how often do we write this all down and analyse it? This is the function of the Dialogue Box before you approach your internal audience.

What follows is a fictional case study about a manufacturing organization; let's call it Nirvana Manufacturing Corporation.

Intelligence

Nirvana has recently been formed out of a merger, and they have revised their compensation and benefits package, which will negatively impact 20 per cent of the workforce, many from one side of the merger but not wholly so. They have to make this unpopular announcement to their employees. The leadership has taken a view on how this translates into their business operations and the demographics of their company. As a result, only a particular section of their workforce is affected, but all employees in the manufacturing plants need to be informed, as they need to know they are not affected. The decision cannot be changed, based on the new business strategy and legal advice the leadership has been given.

The Dialogue Box is going to be used to train Nirvana's managers on how to present this news to their individual manufacturing sites, which are mainly blue collar, with some of the workforce unionized.

This is an unpopular decision affecting 20 per cent of the Nirvana workforce and their compensation and benefits after a recent merger.

FIGURE 10.11 Framing the intelligence

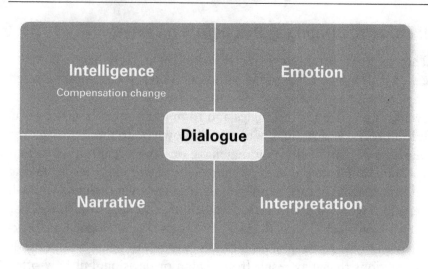

Nirvana is a manufacturing company, struggling to survive and digest a merger that took place during the early stages of recessionary times. The leadership has based its intelligence on a belief that this is one of the actions they need to take in order to thrive, and they have no option to change the decision.

Because not all workers or sites are affected, there is a need to target messages accordingly. However, people talk and employees will know what is happening elsewhere, which can be a cause of concern for employees and the source of many rumours.

In the case of Nirvana, the decision has been taken, the plans put in place. HR has the necessary material they need to manage the changes, and a media release has been prepared. All is ready to go, and the managers have to present the decision, the intelligence, to employees and unions.

Thinking point

When a leadership makes a decision, how much does the leadership account for the emotional impact? Imagine this is your organization; to what extent does your leadership truly engage with the emotional impact of decisions?

Emotion

If we rehearse presenting this intelligence, we can easily imagine there will be a mixed emotional reaction. Generally, we can assume this will be taken as bad news, but those affected will feel the decision is against them, while those unaffected will feel relieved they are okay. Beyond this initial reaction, as the workforce assesses the situation, there will be a sense among employees of unfairness being shown towards their colleagues. Many of those unaffected will step back from their own situation and feel empathy for their affected colleagues, and perhaps feel some anger about what they perceive as an injustice. This will dovetail into anger from the unions on the part of their members.

In issues such as compensation change there tends to be great disparity between leadership and the employee base. Leaders get high pay and bonuses, plus things like share options. They get excited about things like the annual results or the perceived value creation of a merger. This is beyond the interest of many employees, who may be happy the company is doing well because it secures their future in the company, but there are considerable limits to the extent of their excitement. In a situation like this, talking to them about value creation or the annual results is not the most productive, even if the most well-trodden, route to take. The issue needs to be addressed at

FIGURE 10.12 Looking at the emotional impact

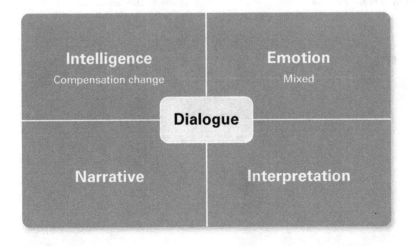

the human level, not just the business level. This is why people are human capital and not just capital.

Thinking point

What is the full range of emotions you can think of in this situation, and what statements can you imagine Nirvana employees making to express these emotions? As Nirvana leadership, how would you react to these emotions and statements?

Interpretation

As the emotions subside, there will be various interpretations of subsequent events. This decision will become part of the company furniture. It becomes the bedrock of rumour. It will shape employee views of events, and foster a sense that this 'could happen to us'. Even if some sites are totally unaffected, rumour can unsettle employees elsewhere, leading them to speculate that this decision could happen in other sites. On another level, there can be speculation that there are plans for other changes as part of the merger integration.

Employees are reading situations subjectively, but framed by the context of the decision announced by Nirvana, and seen through the prism of the emotional response. We can see how the Dialogue Box

FIGURE 10.13   Finding the range of interpretations

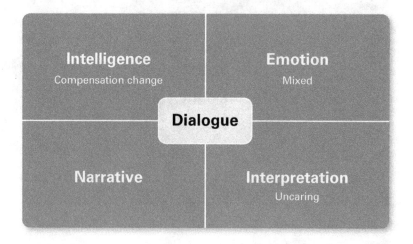

is drawing us through a trajectory that will lead us to the dialogue word that will allow us to think through how we might approach Nirvana employees on the day of the announcement. What has been discerned by Nirvana at this point is that there is a high potential for employees to view the company as uncaring.

Thinking point

What other interpretations do you think could be circulating? If you have been part of a merger or similar unpopular decision, or know people who have talked to you about being in a similar position, can you recall the interpretations circulating around your organization?

Narrative

As various interpretations circulate, there is a narrative that will emerge. As a Nirvana planner, you have to consider what could become the emerging narrative or counter-narrative.

There will be a leadership narrative in any intelligence zone, and in the case of Nirvana the narrative is that the organization has to make changes and stick to the decision to help the company survive and thrive. However, there may be a counter-narrative that this is the thin end of the wedge, as this sort of decision works both ways.

FIGURE 10.14 Locating the dominant narrative

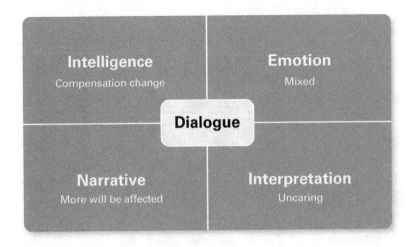

Employees may accept a dominant narrative that what is happening to the company is that it will continue to struggle to survive, but they may counter with a narrative that this decision is the first of many unfavourable decisions for employees. Whether this is true or not it can be taken as the most credible narrative for the time being, and if embraced by employees it will cause morale issues.

We can see from the Dialogue Box that the idea that more employees will be affected will be the narrative for Nirvana to tackle, against a background of mixed emotions and a sense that the leadership is uncaring. How, then, can Nirvana use dialogue to prevent this Dialogue Box trajectory from becoming the reality when they present the announcement to their employees?

Thinking point

What counter-narrative do you think is most likely? Imagine you are Nirvana's leadership; start thinking about how this narrative needs dialogue to ensure your intelligence narrative stays on track when you make the announcement.

Dialogue

You are Nirvana's leadership. As you think through this process, you may come up with many words that will guide you in dialogue. Try these out, and test them to see if they deal with the emotions and

FIGURE 10.15   Dialogue as understanding

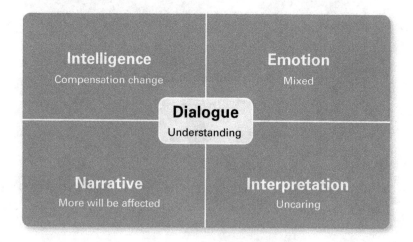

thoughts of your employees. Imagine you are presenting this news; how can you frame the dialogue with the way you announce the news? Imagine also an angry employee bursting into your office, banging their fist on your desk demanding justice. How will you respond?

The trouble is that it is easy to respond in the way we respond to things naturally; our way of handling things. The idea behind the Dialogue Box is that we ensure we have a prepared and productive approach and response. When we are taken by surprise or are under stress we often don't tackle things in a calm way ourselves. This is the point of the Dialogue Box exercise, to think through the scenarios so we are in the right frame of mind to respond to employees who will feel aggrieved.

The word I would be looking for in Nirvana's case is 'understanding'. When you, as a Nirvana leader, make the announcement, the word that can keep you anchored is 'understanding'. You can show you understand the difficulty of the situation, that you are empathetic. If taken by surprise, you can say 'I understand'. You then use this as a way to invite calmer dialogue. At the outset you are recognizing the employee has a point to make and you're prepared to hear it. Ultimately, the decision may not possibly change, but whilst we are quite durable as people and we can grasp the inevitability of a situation, we also desire the dignity of being recognized for our value and the validity of our objections or sense of injustice.

Thinking point

Think through how you handle difficult dialogue situations, and how you might generally deal with these types of situations. Write down how you might change your approach to this kind of situation using the Dialogue Box. In this case the word 'understand' was the word arrived at and used, but if you apply this to your company is 'understand' the word you would arrive at, or is there another word?

II: Using the Dialogue Box after an event

This is the 'horse has bolted' strategy. This section will help you to think through how to change the course of internal communications after an announcement or event has gone astray, to prepare for the angles and to minimize the emotions and get dialogue back on track.

This example is a financial company; let's call it KBO Finance plc. After struggling to effect a merger, the leadership has decided to undertake a reorganization. The CEO will now become president and appoint a new CEO for day-to-day operations. KBO will also relocate the head office building to another part of the city where the headquarters is located. There will be a change in various positions, with some departures as a result. This is all as part of an expansion plan.

In this case, we know what has happened at KBO. The employees understand the intelligence of the situation, but the feedback from them is that they feel unsettled and believe there was a lack of proper engagement. They did not feel consulted on the office move.

Intelligence

A merger reorganization and office relocation are, in the organizational world, the equivalent of a marriage/divorce and house move in private life – very stressful! The challenge for leadership is that there is a long period during merger negotiations where communication is difficult, and employees understand this. However, this does not stop rumours from spreading, and they need to be monitored and tackled as much as is feasible. Once the merger is signed there is a need to start communicating as soon as possible, but often the caution of the

FIGURE 10.16   Reorganizing as the intelligent thing to do

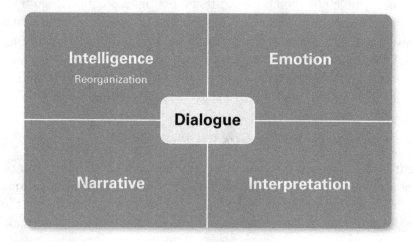

pre-merger phase carries over into the post-merger phase. This is a leadership issue, because there is no such thing in truth as a merger, only friendly and unfriendly takeover battles. As the dust starts to settle, the management knows there will be only one CEO, one head of finance, one head of communications, one head of sales, etc. And many of these changes are only settled after the agreement is signed. The leadership, in getting all caught up in the 'heat of battle' as they seek to win the day, must remember their employees, for they are the ones who will win the peace.

Thinking point

Given the need for secrecy and confidentiality in a merger, how can leadership communicate in a meaningful way to employees, without being banal or fuelling even more speculation?

Emotion

People recognize the logic of a merger reorganization, but the impact remains one of being unsettled. Employees want to know what the effect will be on them, and where they fit. Will their boss change? Will they lose colleagues, or even their own job? As changes are made there will be emotion around those changes, especially if a popular boss leaves or people lose their jobs. There will be pent-up emotion,

FIGURE 10.17 Mixing up the emotions

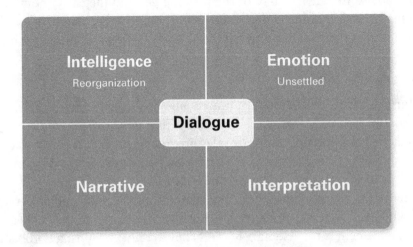

which has built up over the merger period. If information has leaked out during the merger this can create emotional issues.

The background to this is that KBO has already been through a long period of merger negotiations, which means there are latent emotions that will surface. The emotions will quickly grasp the rumours already circulating and add this into the potentially explosive mix. You need to assess therefore the situation that is pre-existing, and not just look at this announcement as one that will create an emotional response; it may only be the trigger for pent-up frustration.

Once the merged partners get together there will be suspicion on both sides, each believing oddly that the other is the threat. In this new organization people can feel alienated. This atmosphere can be explosive, which is why something like two-thirds of all mergers fail. One of the events that tends to settle the noise substantially is the presentation of the new organization chart, where everyone can begin to see how it all fits together. This process can take a while, but it is important to get this organization chart to employees at the earliest opportunity. The creation of a new brand around the new organization is also a great opportunity to address emotional issues by getting all employees looking at a new identity and set of objectives based on the new future the merger seeks to co-create.

Thinking point

You are the KBO leadership; what communications approach would you advise for the first day of the new merger and the early months? What messages can effectively address rumours on the one hand, and inspire confidence and energy for the newly merged entity on the other?

Interpretation

During mergers there is, as pointed out above, huge potential for rumours. Who's going, who's leaving? Will it go through, will it fail? Finance is having problems, or sales are not so good in the new partnership. All of these questions and viewpoints shape the interpretation of employees as they witness events in the company. These interpretations are views they share with others outside, and are grist to the mill for the competition. There will be complaints, such as, 'Management is not listening to us', 'They are not consulting with us',

FIGURE 10.18 Disconnecting the interpretations

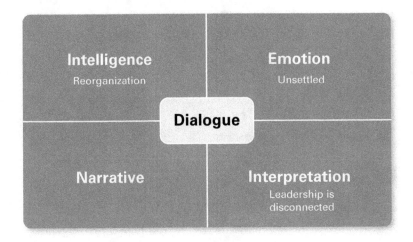

and, 'There are all these consultants running about asking the same questions; can't we just get on with our work?' Two people in a meeting can be interpreted as a sign one of them is on their way out, or some other such thing. One direction this can go is a sense that the leadership is disconnected from the employee base, not understanding the impact of the merger and the decisions being taken about the office move.

Thinking point

Can you distinguish between powerful interpretations versus idle speculation or mischief-making? Quite often leadership can be persuaded by a wrong interpretation, so why is that? How do we figure out what is persuasive and what is not?

Narrative

If we get a theme running through the interpretation of events by employees that the senior leadership is out of touch with the employee base then this can lead to a sense that the employee is not valued. They are treated simply as pawns in a corporate chess game, or fodder for financial wheeling and dealing. This will disconnect them from the vision of the merger. In the case of KBO Finance, this is a white-collar workforce that is of a size that they feel they are owed

FIGURE 10.19 Evaluating the narrative

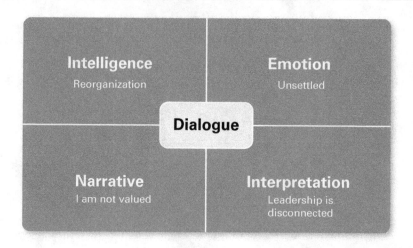

more than they are getting from their leadership. The dominant narrative here is that the employee is not valued, unlike the assets gained through the merger. The merger aimed at growth and a vision of the future now meets a counter-narrative that employees are not an important or integral part of the merger vision. The environment has become quite dysfunctional. All the communications and messaging from leadership speak of a bright future together and the importance of the employees, but their actions in the wake of the merger and what is perceived as a cavalier manner in which the HQ is relocated belies their message.

Thinking point

Why does the leadership in an organization get it wrong and present a narrative that finds a counter-narrative arising from employees? What factors would you highlight in a merger such as KBO Finance? Do you think the leadership is quick to grasp a counter-narrative, or does it simply learn the hard way?

Dialogue

We have a situation at KBO Finance that finds the narrative being challenged by a strong counter-narrative. What word will help KBO get back on track? To answer this we have to look at the unsettled nature of the employees and the various interpretations, and in this

FIGURE 10.20 Trust the dialogue

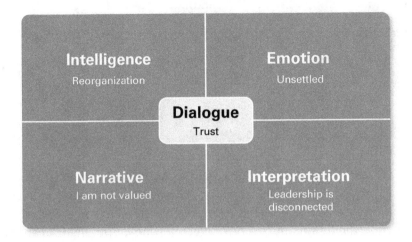

Intelligence	Emotion
Reorganization	Unsettled

Dialogue
Trust

Narrative	Interpretation
I am not valued	Leadership is disconnected

case the word we can come to is trust. The leadership has lost the trust of employees, and needs to regain and build that trust. They should acknowledge there is a trust issue, and use that word to anchor discussions. This means explaining the ways in which trust has been betrayed, and opportunities located for having discussions around trust.

III: Using a Dialogue Box exercise

Here is a last exercise before you tackle the Dialogue Box in your organization. The event is one common enough in an organization. You have the idea now, so given this breakdown of intelligence, emotion, interpretation and narrative, what dialogue would you plan to have?

Intelligence

The intelligence is a new IT rollout, which the IT department is very excited about. It is a new document management system, which is important but not one that affects everyone and will not necessarily grab the rapt attention of your organization.

For this exercise, take an organization you've worked in at some point in the past, not your current organization. If you have only worked in your current organization then feel free to use that.

....
....
....
....
....
....

Emotion

The emotion I will posit here is a feeling of confusion and complexity. Would this be true in your case? Use this as your starting point, but write down the range of emotions you recall, and then write in the box what the dominant emotions were and how you would respond to them.

....
....
....
....
....
....

FIGURE 10.21 What dialogue will *you* choose?

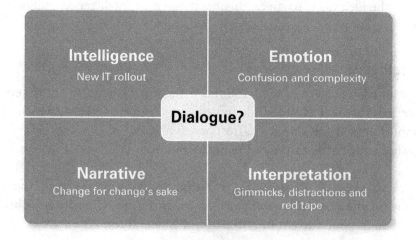

Interpretation

I am giving you here a dominant interpretation, which is that whatever the IT function communicates it will be met with resistance, with people interpreting the communication as comprising gimmicks, distractions and red tape. Again, is this true in your example? Write down the reactions and how you would respond to them.

....

....

....

....

....

....

Narrative

The narrative I suggest will come out of this situation is one that this is all change for change's sake, and will be a negative for the IT department, which is attempting to make people's life easier with the new system. Does your narrative get defined this way, or have you located a different narrative? Write down the narrative and how you would respond to it.

....

....

....

....

....

....

Dialogue

You now have all your elements in place, and it is time to define what dialogue you need to have. This will depend upon how major you see the disconnect to be, and it may be that you in fact arrive at a point where this rollout is a smooth one, in which case perhaps your dialogue is one of celebration and figuring out how to use this rollout as a model. So what is your dialogue word, and how will you use it for future discussion?

....

....

....

....

....

....

IV: Using the Dialogue Box in your organization

This is the chance to analyse your own organizational challenges.

Intelligence

Think of a significant event that is going to take place in your organization, and note down your answers to the following questions, taking into account your learnings from this book:

- ✤ What is the event, announcement or action?
- ✤ What is the rationale for doing this?
- ✤ What success factors are defined, or can you define?
- ✤ Have the pitfalls been well defined?

FIGURE 10.22   Using the Dialogue Box in *your* organization

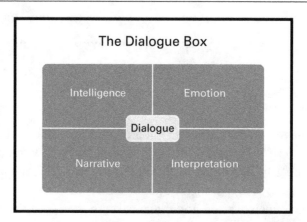

✤ Who is affected?

✤ What is the timeline involved, before, during and after the event?

✤ Are there other questions you need to ask that are not included here?

Define your intelligence:

....

....

....

....

....

....

Emotion

✤ What is the expected or desired emotional response?

✤ What other emotional reactions do you think might result?

✤ Can you break these emotions down into organizational demographics?

✤ Have there been similar situations in the past, and if so what was the emotional response?

✤ Can you make a mind map of the emotional make-up of your organization?

Frame your emotional landscape:

....

....

....

....

....

....

Interpretation

✤ Is there often a sense in your organization that 'management is not listening to us'?

✤ Do employees feel 'management is not consulting with us'?

✤ What levels of trust exist?

✤ How does your communications function communicate with employees, and how would you rate their level of engagement?

✤ Given these answers, what kinds of interpretations can you imagine circulating?

What interpretations are circulating within your organization?

....

....

....

....

....

....

Narrative

✤ What narrative currently exists in the company?

✤ What do employees say about your leadership?

✤ Is there a good connection between the company messaging and the employees, or is there a level of disconnect?

✤ Given this background, what sort of narrative could you imagine emerging from your employee base?

What is the dominant narrative or counter-narrative?

....

....

....

....
....
....

Dialogue

✤ You need to define one word for your dialogue; what word have you arrived at?

✤ How will this word be understood by your employee base?

✤ What lines of dialogue do you see emerging from this single word?

✤ What sentences can you devise for use in your dialogue?

What kind of dialogue do you need to have?

....
....
....
....
....
....

I hope you have successfully arrived at your destination and find the Dialogue Box to be a tool you can use again and again. Remember, the dialogue process you have just been through can be reiterated as the situation changes, and new elements fill the Dialogue Box zones. Dialogue is a continuous process in an organization, and I wish you every success in having a communicating organization that is constantly and constructively in dialogue!

✦ INDEX ✦

Note: page numbers in *italic* indicate figures or tables.

CPSIA information can be obtained
at www.ICGtesting.com
Printed in the USA
JSHW041924040222
22513JS00013B/143

9 780749 478650